NATIONAL STATUTES AND THE LOCAL COMMUNITY

BUILDING CONTROL

National Legislation and the
Introduction of Local Bye-laws
in Victorian England

NATIONAL STATUTES AND THE
LOCAL COMMUNITY

Building Control

National Legislation and the Introduction of Local Bye-laws in Victorian England

S. Martin Gaskell

Assistant Principal, City of Liverpool College of
Higher Education

Published for the
BRITISH ASSOCIATION FOR LOCAL HISTORY
by the
BEDFORD SQUARE PRESS | NCVO

© BALH 1983
ISBN 0 7199 1100 1

First published 1983 by the
BEDFORD SQUARE PRESS of the
National Council for Voluntary Organisations
26 Bedford Square London WC1B 3HU

Printed in England by Henry Ling Ltd, at the Dorset Press, Dorchester, Dorset.

Contents

Illustrations

Table of Legislation (Proposed and Actual) and Related Documents

Date	Government Enquiries and Proposed Legislation	Acts of Parliament	Local Legislation and Controls in Selected Provincial Towns	London Building Regulations
1774				London Building Act
1818			Act for Cleansing, Lighting, Watching and otherwise improving the Town of Sheffield	
1837			Newcastle upon Tyne Act for Regulating and Improving the Borough	
1840	Select Committee Report on the Health of Towns			
1841	Lord Normanby's Bill for the Better Drainage and Improvement of Buildings in Large Towns and Cities			
1842	Select Committee Report on the Regulation of Buildings and the Improvement of Boroughs		Act for Improving the Borough of Leeds	

Date	Government Enquiries and Proposed Legislation	Acts of Parliament	Local Legislation and Controls in Selected Provincial Towns	London Building Regulations
	Report of the Poor Law Commission on the Sanitary Condition of the Labouring Population of Great Britain		Liverpool Building Act	
1844	First and Second Reports of the Royal Commision for Inquiring into the State of Large Towns and Populous Districts		Manchester Borough Police Act	Metropolitan Building Act
1845			Manchester Sanitary Improvement Act	
1847		Towns Improvement Clauses Act		
1848		Public Health Act		
1855		Local Government Act		Act for the Better Local Management of the Metropolis
1858		Local Government Act Office: Form of Bye-Laws		Metropolitan Building Act

1864			Liverpool Sanitary Amendment Act; Building Bye-laws: Sheffield	
1866			Building Bye-laws: Leeds; Building Bye-laws: Newcastle-upon-Tyne	
1867			Building Bye-laws: Manchester	
1869	Royal Sanitary Commission: First Report			
1871	Royal Sanitary Commission: Second Report	Local Government Board established		
1875		Public Health Act		
1877		Local Government Board: Model Bye-laws		
1878				Metropolis Management and Building Acts Ammendment Act 1878
1882				Metropolis Management and Building Acts Amendment Act 1882
1883			Sheffield Corporation Act	
1889			Sheffield New Bye-laws	
1894				London Building Act

Foreword

This book is one of a series (initiated by the Standing Conference for Local History and now sponsored by the British Association for Local History) dealing with specific statutes and their effect on local communities. The situation prior to enactment of these statutes is described, together with the means of their enforcement and the implications for local communities of the time. Reference is also made to the documentary evidence available to the local historian of today.

The series is under the joint honorary editorship of Mr J. J. Bagley, MA, FRHistSoc, formerly Reader in History, Institute of Extension Studies, University of Liverpool, and Mrs Jennifer Kermode, BA, Research Lecturer in the Departments of Medieval and Modern History, University of Liverpool.

The exercise of their editorial role calls for knowledge, understanding and a willingness to contribute—in whatever measure may be required—from their resources of time and energy. Gratitude is expressed to them for their work, and to the author of this particular title for the preparation of his material.

Acknowledgements

Particular thanks are due to Dr Roger Harper for his advice and instruction, to Graham Davies and Robert Thorne for their constructive criticism at an early stage, and to the Editors for their patient attention to detail.

Introduction

The purpose of this book is to examine the evolution and establishment of building bye-laws as the means of controlling building and urban development. The pressing need for such control arose in the eighteenth century with the expansion of urban areas, though building regulations as such had a long history in this country, dating back at least to 1189. The industrialisation and urbanisation of the early nineteenth century extended this need, and created the circumstances within which building controls were extended. Inevitably this development was closely related to the public health movement and to contemporary pressures for housing and building reform. This book, however, is a study of building regulation as a phenomenon in its own right, and of the legislative and administrative system concerned with the control of new building development.

The book concentrates on the period from 1840 to 1880 because it was in this relatively short period that rudimentary regulations were shown to be inadequate, and professional opinion and government action together occasioned a dramatic change in the scope of building regulations as well as in the manner of their formulation and presentation. It is not concerned to examine in detail the content of different codes, whether national or local, or to compare standards applied in different places and at different times with respect to particular aspects of building development. The intention is rather to analyse the emergence of the legal and administrative system under which effective and extensive controls were made enforceable.

This was a slow process and cannot be related to one single piece of legislation. It was the result of a series of practical responses to a developing situation, and of the achievement of an appropriate balance between local interests and central intervention. In that process, however, the Local Government Act of 1858 has a central and crucial significance. The first chapter therefore examines the response of local and national government to the social and sanitary problems of early Victorian England prior to that Act. The central section of the book examines the legislation of 1858 and the presentation of the first set of model bye-laws by the government. The third and final chapter involves a number of local studies,[1] in order to look at the effect of these legislative and administrative changes on local authorities and their organisation of building controls, and at the consolidation of this piecemeal process of growth in the Public Health Act of 1875 and the Model Bye-laws of 1877. By then the main building regulations that were considered essential for the safety of the general public had been established, and the method of their operation had been resolved as a delicate balance between local and central government.

I Building and Sanitary Problems in Early Victorian England

The Common Law of England in the early period of our history provided but very scantily for the rude and scattered population of the country in regard to their social exigencies, and though the expansive powers of modern jurisprudence extend the principles of that law very far to meet the demands of the civilised state of this densely-peopled nation, still those principles must be maintained generally upon the basis of their original foundations.[2]

By the 1880s local authorities had the right to frame bye-laws for a particular town to control a whole range of local and detailed problems. George Chambers, writing in 1883 on the law relating to public health and local government, identified twenty-four categories of such bye-laws, including: the management of burial grounds; tramways; hackney carriages; public walks and pleasure grounds; the management of public libraries and museums; the control of lodging houses and artisan dwellings; markets; the prohibition of offensive trades; baths and washhouses; the prevention of nuisances arising from filth and rubbish; the level and construction of streets; the ventilation, drainage and construction of new buildings.[3] Such bye-laws were local in their origin and operation. They were additional to statute law for, though parliament was the supreme legislative body, it could not administer the law. Bye-laws were therefore the means of allowing the application in detail of a general statute; as such they could not be made without due obligation to the law of the land. The bye-law made it possible to apply a general enabling statute, in order to meet the particular needs of a local community.

This system, as it had developed by the end of the nineteenth century, reflected not only the division of powers between the legislative and administrative functions of government, but more particularly the subtle balance of powers which had evolved in England between central and local government. With a society mistrustful of central authority, the bye-law became the means of local control of the social policy laid down by the State, in permissive and later obligatory legislation. Their establishment was part of the development of the Victorian welfare state which, lacking any preconceived philosophy, evolved as a practical response to specific problems. The system of bye-laws that characterised English local government by the end of the nineteenth century reflected the practical way in which government had coped with the social problems of the Industrial Revolution.

Hitherto the primary feature of local government had been the reliance which it had placed on local initiative. From the mid-eighteenth century through into the first decade of the nineteenth century, as population increased, special legislation was used to extend the means of improving the external conditions of towns or regulating the conduct of persons in their outdoor life. Up to the 1830s it was assumed that any such action that tampered with established rights and thus required legal sanction would originate within the particular circumstances of a locality and be applicable to it alone. This type of legislation had a long history. It had dealt originally with matters such as the settling of estates, but had later been used to meet the problems created by the social conditions of industrialisation. Peculiar to each locality, such local and private Acts were sometimes of a limited character and at other times of a very comprehensive nature. One town might seek to provide the means of improving its streets and its sewers; another might seek to obtain adequate means of lighting its highways; another to establish an efficient police force or to set up and regulate markets. All or several objectives might be combined in one bill.

Each bill was presented separately to Parliament by a particular locality on its own initiative. For example, in 1837 a local Act gave the Mayor, Aldermen and Burgesses of Newcastle-upon-Tyne the power to repair streets and other highways, while in the following year Sheffield secured powers for making new streets or thoroughfares and widening and improving others.[4] There was no general measure provided for the country until 1845. It was inevitable, however, that over a period local Acts should tend to conform to a pattern in their provisions and presentation. During the eighteenth century, local improvement legislation was intended to improve the external condition of towns or to regulate the conduct of persons in their outdoor life. Such local Acts provided for paving, cleansing, watching and lighting, and the control of nuisances and obstructions in streets.[5] Endeavours of this kind had characterised the London Improvement Act of 1662[6] and were adopted elsewhere much later in the eighteenth century. The concern for safety and convenience in centres of growing population led inevitably to legislation which tried to control individual buildings as they impinged on the street and its users, dealing variously with the control of cellar flaps, steps, projecting porches and windows. From these attempts to prevent obstructions and dangerous features in buildings which could harm passers-by, it was a logical development to legislation which sought to direct the pattern and position of new building so as to make it more convenient and secure for the whole community. By the late eighteenth century local improvement Acts were frequently providing authorities with the rudimentary means of controlling the foundations and elevations of buildings, their guttering and piping, and their siting in relation to the streets of the town. These were not controls which related to matters of health. They did not attempt to regulate the amount of open space around a building, the width of streets or the height of buildings or rooms. Neither were they conceived of as regulations concerned with aesthetic standards, though individually they might well have encouraged the standardisation of style which accorded well with the character of Georgian architecture. Essentially eighteenth century building regulations, as they emerged through local improvement Acts, covered matters of safety and convenience—the limitation of the risk of fire, the restriction of encroachment into streets and the control of dangerous structures.

Such regulation was at its most developed in eighteenth century London where the various building regulations following the Great Fire were codified in the London Building Act of 1774.[7] In addition to laying down standards for structure and safety, comparable with other contemporary building regulations, the London Act was also of considerable significance, in that it established through the District Surveyors an effective machinery for control. Reflecting the significance of London in the urban hierarchy, these metropolitan regulations were to provide a model and guide for later developments in provincial towns.

Though such local legislation was often quite comprehensive in its coverage, it was necessarily limited in its effectiveness. Not all local Acts applied to an entire district; they often referred just to a particular group of buildings or estates. In various towns there were flagrant examples of conflicting jurisdictions causing great confusion and inefficiency. In Liverpool there were two sets of Commisioners as well as the Town Council with powers over sewer-

1 Terrace of the 1820s in Kennington Road, London. *(GLC Historic Buildings Photograph Collection)*

age and paving. To a large extent these independent authorities had concurrent jurisdiction which could not be exercised without clashing. Similarly in Birmingham there were several distinct bodies of Commissioners exercising power under various local statutes, and also four independent boards of surveyors. In Manchester the townships were under distinct jurisdictions and only four had local Acts. All these authorities administered limited areas for drainage purposes, and these comprised only a part of their natural and proper drainage area. Thus Manchester in 1845 was subdivided into jurisdictions, partly municipal and partly parochial, totally inconsistent with any natural limits for drainage. The situation was similar in Bradford, Halifax and Leeds.

In many other developing urban centres, building regulations did not take in many of the areas which were growing most rapidly in population. Much new building therefore escaped control, and construction was permitted of whole districts of unwholesome and unhealthy buildings. Moreover, many authorities were securing separate, local building Acts for much the same purposes. Between the years 1800 and 1845 nearly 400 improvement Acts were obtained for various aspects of local government and some sanitary purposes in 208 towns in England and Wales.[8] Inevitably there was some variation in detail between all these legislative measures, and this led to a considerable increase in litigation; in particular, the sanctions relating to similar objects varied in different Acts. At the same time, the expense of securing separate local legislation was an increasing burden, both in terms of cost and parliamentary time. The Hammonds have estimated that it cost each authority something in the order of £2,000 to secure a local Act, though in some instances the outlay was much greater with costs reaching between £10,000 and £12,000 for obtaining some special legislation.⁹ Yet although the requirements of towns were really very similar, local Acts remained the standard procedure in most matters, certainly with regard to building regulations. It was the great legislative work of the 1830s with its recourse to general Acts which questioned the basic assumptions underlying local initiative and direction in legislation. The Royal Commission on Municipal Corporations of 1837–8 criticised the need for each town to produce its own regulations on matters which were of public concern and applicable to every town in the kingdom.

There was then growing public recognition that the problems associated with town life were not confined to a few industrial centres or to obscure and congested districts of dirt and disease. By the 1840s it was becoming clear that sanitary deficiencies were in fact very general, and as the second report of the Royal Commission on the State of Large Towns noted in 1845, 'The most important evils affecting the public health throughout England and Wales are characterised by little variety, and it is only in the degree of their intensity that the towns exhibit the worst examples of such ill.'¹⁰ The bigger towns were the growing points of the new society and it was there it had to tackle the complex tasks which made it possible for large numbers to live together. Since the eighteenth century the pace of urban growth had, almost inevitably, been accompanied by insanitary housing conditions which had in turn increased the national death rate. The effects of rapid population growth and un-controlled building in towns provided a poor foundation on which to build an urban way of life.

Through the 1830s and 1840s a series of government inquiries, along with the work of medical and statistical societies, made clear to Parliament and to middle class electors the conditions in which the poor were living: the frequent lack of water and drainage in towns; the dangers of the sub-division of old decaying property; the problems created with the shoddy new houses thrown up in back-courts or new suburbs; and the inadequacy of the uncleansed and airless streets. It was a state of affairs which affected not only the poor, and the outbreak of cholera in 1831 alarmed, if only temporarily, those in control in society. The scale and implications of the problem had to be impressed on government, both local and central, before the traditional antipathy to action and reluctance to interfere with vested property rights could be overcome.

The official reports and inquiries were mainly to identify, investigate and ameliorate the dirt, disease and squalor which had intensified to a level which threatened social stability and which appeared with something of the force of novelty. In the first instance, these investigations were only concerned with buildings, and more particularly with houses as places where overcrowding transmitted disease or where the lack of water or sanitation discouraged cleanliness and modesty. The public health reports were important, however, in that they drew attention to the need for a greater degree of building control if the sanitary condition of towns was to be improved. In the first place, they pointed to the worst excesses of uncontrolled and unregulated working class housing; secondly, the connection between health and building control was tentatively demonstrated. The nature of the housing revealed was not in itself new. The court system, cellar dwellings and back-to-backs were an inheritance from pre-industrial towns. What was evident by the 1830s was the intensity of the pressure on available accommodation and the failure of speculative builders to meet the mass demand for urban working class housing. Investigation after investigation spelt out the consequences of uncontrolled development.[11] The nature and quality of building construction was described in detail, as in this classic extract from Chadwick's report of 1842:

> An immense number of small houses occupied by the poorer classes in the suburbs of Manchester are of the most superficial character . . . new cottages are erected with a rapidity that astonishes persons who are unacquainted with their flimsy structure. They have certainly avoided the objectionable mode of forming underground dwellings, but have run into the opposite extreme, having neither cellar nor foundation. The walls are only half brick thick, or what the bricklayers call 'brick noggin', and the whole of the materials are slight and unfit for the purpose . . . they are built back-to-back; without ventilation or drainage: and, like a honeycomb, every particle of space is occupied.[12]

Working class housing had become a 'problem'. Moreover, it had been identified as a problem not just in terms of the quality of its construction but also because of the social and sanitary consequences resulting from that. Many reports noted that the chief evil of bad housing was the sanitary one—the deficient ventilation, the near impossibility of keeping damp floors and walls clean and warm, and the major problems associated with the disposal of refuse. In Liverpool, Dr Duncan reported in 1842 on badly built cellars which were so wet that the inhabitants had to take the door off its hinges and lay it on the floor supported by bricks. Two years later in Manchester, Engels described how in Little Ireland water was constantly welling up through house floors.[13] Contemporary medical reformers argued that because of these conditions bad housing was the breeding ground of disease and especially epidemics. Though the contagionists and miasmatists were to argue for many years as to how that disease was actually transmitted there was no doubt that there was a relationship between fever and filth.[14] The consequences of an uncontrolled and unregulated environment for the growing mass of urban poor were assessed and analysed in these numerous reports and investigations, both nationally and locally, during the 1830s and 1840s, and out of the conviction that insanitary conditions threatened the health of society and through that its wealth and stability, the campaign for public health was born.

Inherent in that campaign was the belief that the poverty of the physical environment of the urban poor was not inevitable and that the conditions under which they lived were neither necessarily their own fault nor under their control. From this basis it was then argued that some form of public intervention and control was necessary, and so came about in many towns the provision of unpolluted water, the control of obnoxious trades, the restriction of overcrowding, as well as the essential regulation of buildings and of town growth. Despite traditional resistance to any such controls, local authorities had to face the necessity for them and the question of how to make them effective. Quite clearly, existing local Acts, even where they were in operation, were frequently unable to cope with the intensity and rapidity of current urban expansion. Apart from the fact that they usually covered only a very limited range of building problems, they were frequently so badly drafted that the powers they did provide were often not enforceable. For example, in 1844 and 1845 two cases were brought by individuals against authorities challenging the definition of a 'house' as used in local Acts; it was not clear, for example, whether the term 'house' included buildings which could be used as dwelling houses though they had not been built as such or other buildings such as stables with accommodation over them. Such lack of clarity and precision with regard to the terminology of local Acts meant that they frequently could not be enforced for the purposes for which they were intended. The Public Health movement promoted the idea of extending the Building Acts to embrace matters of health and pointed out the need for such Acts to be widely applicable and readily enforceable.

Attention was focused on the connection between health and building control by Southwood Smith in 1839 in the fifth report of the Poor Law Commission[15] and was followed through in a series of subsequent reports and enquiries. In giving evidence to the Royal Commission on the State of Large Towns, he pleaded the case for a national building Act:

> Whatever regulations are made for one part of the country should be made for all, as far as it may be found practicable to devise measures which can be carried out in all. I should rejoice to see the present prevalent system of separate local acts abandoned. If there are certain regulations which are required for the whole country, and of this every fresh enquiry affords additional evidence, then such regulations should be made universal, and if local acts are retained, at all, their enactments should consist of regulations expressly adapted to each respective locality, in accordance with the great general regulations, and subservient to giving practical effect to them.[16]

Meanwhile, the Select Committee on the Health of Towns reported in 1840, and among its main recommendations was the proposal for a general building Act which would be the responsibility of central government and which would be applicable to all larger towns.[17] Administratively such a measure would overcome the difficulties encountered with individual local Acts and would not be restricted to a particular area. However, it was proposed that such a general building Act would be limited to the control of lower class housing and to the prevention of forms of construction incompatible with health. The Committee considered that these included cellar dwellings, unless they had areas in the front and back and drains, rows of houses erected in close courts built up at the end and rows of dwellings built back-to-back so as to prevent any through ventila-

2 A court in central Liverpool before the 1842 Improvement Act. *(Liverpool City Libraries)*

tion. In addition, the Committee felt it would be appropriate to require that a certain amount of space should be left open both before and behind every row of houses, though it did not recommend how extensive that space should be and whether it should be directly related to the height of the houses concerned.[18] Likewise, the Committee suggested that there should be sufficient underground drainage, provision of conveniences and receptacles for refuse that would allow for comfort and cleanliness in working class homes. The inclusion of such provisions was quite novel for a building Act which had been traditionally concerned with the strength of walls, dangerous projections and protection from fire. With these proposals, therefore, the Select Committee signalled the transition of building regulations from being purely structural in concern to being, in addition, agents of sanitary and social control.

A change of this nature inevitably threatened vested interests, and the Committee was very aware that if the proposals were to be acceptable, then they should interfere as little as possible with private property and should certainly not do so any more than was strictly necessary. Whilst the Committee recognised the necessity for intervention in the interests of general well being, especially amongst those who could not protect themselves, it showed traditional respect for the sanctity of private property and the right of the individual to manage his own property. In this sense, it reflected the philosophical tensions and inherent contradictions underlying the development of Victorian building regulations. For while contemporaries generally held to a belief that *laissez-faire* represented the most desirable social and political ideology, they had to accept that the problems posed by urban industrial society of necessity required the intervention of the state. The revelations of the Select Committee enquiring into the Health of Towns had considerable influence on the Government, and Lord Normanby, the Home Secretary in Melbourne's second administration, introduced a bill in 1841 for the better drainage and improvement of buildings in large towns and cities.[19] The proposed building Act was to apply to all the Borough Councils as defined under the Municipal Corporation Act of 1835,[20] including those in Ireland and Scotland, though certain sections would not be operative in London and other provincial towns which already had their own Acts covering fire hazards and the structure and stability of buildings. Following the second reading, the bill was divided and a separate 'Building Regulations Bill' was drawn up which restricted itself to the range of topics dealt with in the existing London Building Act.[21] This bill was, however, postponed as a result of the change of Government and was sent to a Select Committee of the House of Lords in 1842 for examination, and then eventually withdrawn.[22] But although the bill never passed into law, the debate surrounding its passage was important in the development of building regulations.

In particular, Lord Normanby's bill and the Select Committee drew attention to the need for strengthening regulations concerning the structure of buildings and the need to extend those covering ventilation and space around buildings. It brought to proposed national legislation the long established requirement in the Building Acts of London that the walls should be of 'good, sound, well burnt bricks or good sound stone, properly bonded and set in good mortar or cement'. It proposed also that parapets and party walls should project above the level of the roof which was generally accepted as an effective means of preventing the spread of fire. Compared with some local Acts, however, the bill was less strict about the thickness of chimneys or the closeness of timbers to flues. Similarly, while the bill indicated the need for footings in the form of stepped brickwork in conjunction with the schedule for wall thickness, it did not include specifications for foundations or damp courses. These points, along with the proposals concerning ventilation and the space around buildings, reflected a somewhat cautious approach to the problems. Whereas the original bill included a clause preventing back-to-back houses, this did not feature in the latter proposals. The bill, however, intended to establish controls to prevent the creation of alleys and courts that were built up at the end so as to prevent through ventilation. At the same time, it was proposed that there should be a minimum street width of 30 ft for 'carriage-ways' and 20 ft for those designated as 'foot passages'. But in these proposals neither the width of streets nor the amount of open space to be left around buildings were directly related to the height of the buildings involved, which limited the effectiveness of these clauses. The Normanby Bill thus continued the tradition of eighteenth century building regulations, but associated with this certain innovatory health controls allowing for the circulation of air within and around buildings. Hitherto, the emphasis in building regulations had been on the prevention of structural collapse and the restriction of the spread of fire. With these proposals, building regulations began to change from concern simply for protection to involvement with the improvement of buildings and of the environment.

Such advances could not be achieved, however, without over-coming the distrust and dislike of any extension of centralised con-trol. The bill was subject to considerable criticism both in the press and from witnesses before the Select Committee; it was this in part which prevented its passage into law. And this criticism provides the historian with a very clear insight into contemporary attitudes towards regulatory controls and towards building Acts in general. Then, as now, the argument was advanced that any extension of rules and procedures would deter those who traditionally invested in property and that as a result the supply of buildings would be diminished. In petitions to the Select Committee the Owners and Occupiers of Building Land in Manchester and Salford complained that the scale of fees proposed for surveyors would involve them in unreasonable expense and the Owners and Occupiers of Houses in Liverpool argued that the 'irresponsible' regulations would put builders to 'great trouble' and thus directly increase the cost of houses and so adversely affect the rents of the working classes.[23] Many provincial commentators assessed the effect on the cost of buildings of the introduction of such legislation, claiming the restrictions on court dwellings and back-to-backs would limit the number of houses possible on a site, while regulations on the structure of walls and roofs would add considerably to the cost of working class houses. Anything that increased the cost of such houses would throw additional burdens of expense on the tenants, who would then be able to afford less in the way of accommodation. This economic conundrum was to prove a continuing problem for nineteenth century housing reformers. At the same time, many witnesses did not feel regulations were necessarily appropriate for all types of property, and they instanced those clauses concerned with limiting the spread of fire as being very suitable for the large scale buildings of the metropolis, but too elaborate for the smaller scale working class housing.

Alongside this questioning of whether the bill could actually achieve its desired objectives, there was a more general concern about the way in which the bill would extend the influence of central control. Witness after witness argued before the Select Committee that their native towns and cities were currently operating adequate and effective regulations of buildings and that they would not benefit from such a bureaucratic imposition. Increasing interference with the rights of private property was not welcomed by the representatives of local power and politics, any more than they approved of the subordination of local interests to national control. For not only did the bill have anomalies and shortcomings in its drafting, but more seriously it paid inadequate attention to the variations in building techniques and traditions in different areas. As a piece of national legislation it was insufficiently flexible and it highlighted the problems inherent in any attempt to control building development on a national basis.

The proposals in Lord Normanby's bill were very much in the metropolitan tradition, and it is not surprising that following its defeat a new bill which incorporated some of the innovations previously proposed was brought forward for London. The Metropolitan Building Act of 1844 extended the area which was controlled by such an Act and strengthened the powers of the district surveyors.[24] It followed Lord Normanby's bill in its combination of certain health controls with the traditional pattern of building regulations in London; it introduced for the first time controls relating to streets and spaces around buildings, drainage and ventilation, as well as controls affecting structure and safety. Perhaps the most significant development was the inclusion of a regulation which related the width of a street to the height of the adjoining building, allowing for a minimum width of 40 ft. Though the regulation included in the Act was not very effective in practice, such a concept had important future implications for both the density of urban development and the planning of towns. Its effect on spatial layout and ventilation was also enhanced by the Act's requirements that all new houses should have backyards and that the minimum area of such a yard should be 100 sq ft. Exceptions were allowed to this regulation, but it effectively prevented back-to-back building in London and established a minimun standard for the lighting and ventilation of all houses. Despite these developments, however, the health controls incorporated in the Act were limited; they did not include the ventilation of foundations and they were at best partial in their imposition of minimim room sizes. The Act did extend, even if somewhat tentatively, drainage controls—limiting the use of cess-pools and regulating the provision of drains. It also enforced a requirement for a certain area of open space to be immediately outside any cellar window. Alongside these innovations in sanitary control, the Metropolitan Building Act attempted to clarify regulations on structure. The Act provided a schedule identifying the thicknesses allowed for foundations and walls in relation to their length and height, the nature of the construction of party walls and their extension above roofs, the rules for openings in external walls and the materials to be used in the construction of chimneys and hearths. While all these structural controls incorporated in the Act were related to traditional methods of building, their specification in a schedule was an important feature which was to be extended in the model bye-laws of the mid-century.

Though in many ways the Metropolitan Building Act of 1844 was conservative in its scope, and though some serious technical problems were to be encountered in its execution, it was nevertheless important in that it placed on the statute book many of the ideas which had developed over the previous decade. At the same time, it was also seen as being a possible prelude to a national measure. The prevailing pressure of reform was directed towards a national building Act. This approach was most clearly articulated by William Hosking, Professor of Architecture at King's College, London,[25] and argued for by the Royal Commission of Enquiry into the State of Large Towns and Populous Districts (1844–45). Every fresh enquiry had shown the need for certain regulations to be in operation throughout the country, and it was felt that it should be possible and practicable to devise general measures which could be carried out in all parts of the country.

In practice, however, each locality still had to secure a separate Act controlling buildings in its own area. Attempts to enact building regulations which could be applied on a national scale had failed; these attempts had highlighted the difficulty of trying to apply a uniform system to all towns and cities. Sanitary reform and environmental control had to be made effective at the local, not the national, level. Before the late 1840s therefore, the initiatives of the large and wealthier towns remained the essential driving force behind practical measures to control the rapidly changing environment. Towns faced with seemingly insuperable problems found no suitable remedy in the sparse general legislation. As Professor Hennock has argued, 'Most of the work of identifying and defining new statutory needs still fell therefore to local authorities, especially in the bigger towns which were in the forefront of the new social experiences'.[26] The years 1836–48 were a great period for local Acts, and it was through these that the developing notions of building regulations and sanitary controls were actually put into practice.

National debates and developments had influenced the thinking behind these local Acts, however, and a survey of some of them indicates the impact in different parts of the country of changes in both the concept and content of building regulations. In 1837, for example, Newcastle-upon-Tyne secured an Act for Regulating and Improving the Borough.[27] Earlier local Acts had provided powers related to the widening and cleansing of streets and the prevention of certain nuisances. This new Act reinforced such traditional powers and introduced controls regulating projections from buildings and encroachments into the streets. The Council required houses to be built in a straight line and attempted at the same time to lay down a building line in relation to the new streets. In addition, the Act introduced certain specifications with respect to the structure of buildings and particularly the thickness of walls and the construction of chimneys. The measures were rudimentary and certainly loosely drafted, but they indicated a concern for at least a basic level of control. When an Act was passed in 1842 for improving the Borough of Leeds,[28] it was the first of the local Acts compelling house drainage to run into a public sewer. The Act forbade the building of any house until a proper drain was made to a sewer, if one was situated within ten yards, and if not to some cesspool within the same distance. Along with this, the Leeds Act brought in the other great tenet of sanitary reform with the imposition of a minimum width of 30 ft for streets that were carriage-ways and of 20 ft for foot-passages. Earlier regulations on projections into streets and dangerous structures were strengthened.

The practical concern of builders and architects with the risk of fire was reflected in the prohibition of thatching, and with the introduction of measures relating to the design and construction of chimneys. At the same time, however, only very hesitant steps were taken to lay down minimum standards for width of closes and alleys and of the openings into them, even though the town was extremely notorious for its crowded yards and back-to-back houses. The main emphasis of the Improvement Act in Leeds was therefore on safety through traditional forms of control, though it did allow for certain essential sanitary regulations. There was a similar balance of interests in the Act passed in 1845 to effect improvements in the Borough of Manchester and for the purpose of promoting the health of its inhabitants.[29] There, though the minimum width of new streets permitted was less than in Leeds, the controls related the height of new buildings and the amount of space around them in the manner of the Metropolitan Building Act.[30] The Manchester Act, like many other local Acts of the period, however, was less than precise in its definition of features such as closes or alleys and was not specific in its definition of prohibitions and penalties. For example, the number of storeys allowed in a house was directly related to the width of the street, but it was not made clear as to whether that width was calculated simply in terms of the roadway or was to include pavements or even gardens. Similarly, the Act included provision for compensation to owners and occupiers whose property was injured by alterations in the level of streets as a result of action under the Act; it did not however specify how that compensation was to be defined or the period within which it would be available. Such measures, while moving in the direction of more effective and comprehensive regulation of buildings, had nevertheless many shortcomings when it came to their practical operation.

These shortcomings were the consequence not simply of local recalcitrance, but were an inevitable outcome of the separate drafting of each private bill by local officials. Though clauses were frequently copied directly from existing Improvement Acts for other towns, there was no means of overall control or consistency in the various local bills as they were presented to Parliament. The procedure was slow and expensive, and as urban legislation increased with the pressure of events, so men recognised the need for general bills which, if sanctioned by Parliament, might be incorporated by reference in each private Act. Certain clauses were identified as essential to good government in every urban community. These provisions and clauses, passed by Parliament in a series of 'Model Acts' between 1845 and 1847, were thus recognised as being fit and proper for adoption by any locality when it sought separate legislation.[31] The matters, which had been the subject of so much private legislation, were classed under distinct heads relating to: purchase of land; provision of markets, gas, water, harbours and piers; paving and cleansing of towns; cemeteries; policing of towns; and the appointment and duties of commissioners. Though there was no measure concerned principally and directly with building regulations, the Towns Improvement Clauses Act of 1847 did incorporate clauses impinging on building matters as they related to the appearance of the town.[32] Streets were therefore one of the main concerns of the Act. Provisions for the control of street widths in conformity with the standards established in Lord Normanby's bill were offered as guides to local authorities. Streets were to be named and numbered. Powers were given for the purchase and removal of buildings in order to improve streets, and for the establishment of building lines. Paving and lighting of streets were catered for at the same time.

With respect to the structure of buildings, the Towns Improvement Clauses Act continued the tradition of the London Building Act that party walls should be carried up through the roof to project at least 12 in at right angles to the slope of the roof, which was to be constructed of incombustible materials. The Act did not include any clauses governing the detailed construction of buildings or the maintenance of proper ventilation and space about buildings. As for the internal quality of houses the only controls were those prohibiting the occupation of cellars and courts and establishing 7 ft as the minimum height for cellar dwellings. Rather, the emphasis was on external features and particularly the provisions for the drainage of surface water in public sewers, along with the proper maintenance of all drains, privies, and cesspools. More generally, following the pattern of the Metropolitan Building Acts, they were to appoint surveyors, inspectors of nuisances and officers of health, as well as to make surveys and maps for districts. In cases where owners were bound to execute improvements, the Act pointed out how expenses might be recovered and the time allowed for repayments, and regulated the levy of rates for sewers and other purposes. It had the added advantage of reducing considerably the length of bills when a local authority could simply make reference to the appropriate clauses in the consolidating Act rather than have to spell out every detail. In the ten years following the introduction of the Clauses Act it was estimated that consolidation had been applied to more than 3,000 private Acts saving some 130,000 pages of print. This greater brevity also allowed for better scrutiny of the bills concerned, as it meant attention could be directed more easily and more quickly to what was special in each case. These were all indications of the development of a more methodical approach to the problems of building control and urban improvement.

But, despite the assistance which this Act provided in the preparation of local Acts, it was still necessary that there should be such local Acts for the introduction of these improvements and regulations into any town. As a consequence, many places which urgently needed such controls did not adopt them because of the continuing expense of securing a local Act, as well as the concern about local opposition. Yet the urban development of the nineteenth century had already created the need for increasingly complex building regulations. The problems of public health and sanitation had faced authorities with the need to move beyond minimal controls for preventing the collapse of buildings, controlling the risk of fire and limiting those nuisances affecting the general public. Against a background of nationally orchestrated concern and criticism, local authorities had reacted to changing circumstances in a series of *ad hoc* measures which responded to particular local characteristics and conditions. The failure of proposals for a national building Act had emphasised the need to cater for such local interests and variations in practice. Such reliance on local initiatives had not resulted by the late 1840s, however, in a generally effective system of control, either from a structural or a sanitary point of view, despite the increase in the scope of local building regulations. It was in responding to this situation, against a background of tension generated by local mistrust of the development of any central controlling agency, that the legislative base was established between 1848 and 1858 for the more effective enforcement of building controls based on a locally administered structure of building bye-laws.

II The Local Government Act 1858 and the First Model Bye-laws

Despite the growing sophistication of building controls, there had been only a limited achievement and partial application of local building regulations in practice during the first few decades of the nineteenth century. The Second Report of the Royal Commission on the State of Large Towns, for example, reported that no rapid improvement in the condition of buildings in the most densely crowded districts could be expected. But despite the failure to tackle the problems hitherto, the Commission argued that it should be relatively simple to prevent similar evils from recurring in the future through legislation which regulated buildings and street widths, ensured proper drainage and paving, and gave central government the power to inspect the execution of all general sanitary regulations in large towns.

Pressure of this kind for an extension of health controls was reinforced by a 'more potent propagandist', the cholera epidemic of 1848. Though most local authorities viewed with concern the prospect of a growth in central control or authority, events increased public support for reform on such a basis. The resultant Public Health Act of 1848 marked a landmark in social reform.[33] The Act established national standards for the operation and responsibilities of local authorities in the field of public health. As such it provided the first almost complete code of public health. The effectiveness of the measure in practice was, however, limited since the Act was permissive in character, rather than obligatory. Except when the death rate was higher than 23 per 1,000 the Act empowered but did not compel local health boards to pursue sanitary reform. Moreover, the General Board of Health established under the Act could not compel a town to take any effective action since it had no powers of inspection; it was in essence an advisory and supervisory body, rather than a source of authority and initiative. The Act was however of considerable importance in the developing pattern of social legislation because it enabled local boards to make bye-laws relating to public health. Its code could be adopted without the expense of obtaining a local Act, and its implementation could be reinforced by the appointment of Medical Officers of Health.

The content of the Public Health Act was only marginally to do with the control of buildings and the layout of towns; it was primarily concerned with the provision of drains and water supply, and secondly with the paving and cleansing of streets. It did allow for the control of streets and buildings, but only at the complete discretion of the local authority. In the context of public health, therefore, it enabled the control of cellars and privies, specifically embodying the basic requirement in the London Building Act for there to be doors to privies in newly erected or rebuilt houses. It also incorporated the provisions of the Towns Improvement Clauses Act affecting drains for houses and their connection to sewers and cesspits. The Public Health Act also adopted from several local Acts, especially the Liverpool Building Act of 1842,[34] regulations concerning the through ventilation of courts and alleys. These constructional concerns were, however, peripheral to the main emphasis of the Act and were included only as permissive powers.

By 1854 only 182 Boards had been established under the Public Health Act, and very few of these had concerned themselves with building control. Clearly effective regulation of buildings needed stronger provisions for inspection and enforcement—further interference by central government officials in the affairs of local communities. The Act however, had been another step towards the establishment of certain administrative and legislative procedures which were to be the pattern for further building regulations. In 1858, with a minority Tory Government in office, Parliament amended the Public Health Act of 1848 to make further provision for the local government of towns and populous districts, with the passage of the Local Government Act.[35] This Act extended the powers introduced in the Public Health Act of 1848 for local authorities to excecute bye-laws. In effect, it meant that the range of provisions embodied in the Towns Improvement Clauses Act were now available to towns and cities without having to secure a private local Act. The limited attention in the Public Health Act given to the control of buildings was now considerably extended in order to include regulations for the structure and stability of buildings, the space around them, and the control of fire. The Local Government Act, therefore, while it was in many ways an imperfect piece of legislation, constituted a measure of central significance in the legislative and administrative development of building regulations in this country. It enabled local authorities to make bye-laws to control buildings and streets which were as constructive and comprehensive as those to be found in the best of contemporary local building Acts.

These powers were provided for in Section 34 of the Local Government Act which enabled every local board to make bye-laws with respect to the following matters:

1. with respect to the level, width and construction of new streets and the provisions for the sewerage thereof;
2. with respect to the structure of walls of new buildings for securing stability and the prevention of fires;
3. with respect to the sufficiency of the space about buildings to secure a free circulation of air and with respect to the ventilation of buildings;
4. with respect to the drainage of buildings, to water closets, privies, ash-pits and cesspools in connection with buildings and to the closing of buildings or parts of buildings unfit for human habitation, and to the prohibition of their use for such habitation.

And they may further provide for the observance of the same by enacting therein such provisions as they think necessary, as to the giving of notices, as to the deposit of plans and sections by persons intending to lay out new streets or to construct buildings, as to inspection by the local Board, and as to the power of the local Board to remove, alter or pull down any work begun or done in contravention of such bye-laws; provided always that no such bye-laws shall affect any building erected before the date of the constitution of the District. But for the purposes of this Act the re-erecting of any buildings pulled down to or below the ground floor or the conversion into a dwelling house of any building not originally constructed for human habitation, or the conversion into more than one dwelling house of a building originally constructed as one dwelling house only, shall be considered the erection of a new building.

This section broadened the range of regulations affecting buildings and streets, as compared with the Public Health Act of 1848. Alongside this legislative development went changes in the character of central control with the abolition of the General Board of Health. Under the Public Health Act of 1858,[36] the Medical Officer to the former Board was transferred to the Privy Council, while the residual activity of the State with regard to town improvement was developed in a sub-department of the Home Office formed in 1858 and called the Local Government Act Office. Many contemporaries, and indeed supporters of the Act, hoped that these measures would serve to decentralise the whole system of health administration by relieving local authorities of the necessity of referring to a central Board in London. In practice, however, as Royston Lambert has argued, 'the basic powers of the centre were unobtrusively and necessarily preserved in use and in some areas largely extended'.[37] In particular, the centre had built up a function and intelligence which the localities, particularly the smaller authorities, could not dispense with; it provided expertise through its professional staff and technical resources. The recognition of this role by the Local Government Act Office was already apparent in 1858 when its Secretary, Tom Taylor, wrote to local boards with reference to a 'Form of Bye-laws' which the Office was preparing. [38] It was the intention that these would serve for the guidance of local boards in the preparation of bye-laws to be submitted for approval in accordance with the Local Government Act. In issuing such a model the Local Government Act Office was conscious of the delicate balance between the centre and the localities inherent in the system of bye-law control; it stressed that these Forms were issued solely in the way of suggestions and that it would be for each board to consider how far the various provisions might be appropriate to their own individual district and what special conditions or modifications might be desirable in each case.

The Form of Bye-laws consolidated the collected experience of several local building Acts, the Metropolitan Building Act of 1855 and the Towns Improvement Clauses Act. It provided, on the basis of Section 34 of the Act, for bye-laws regulating the structure of buildings, streets and the spaces around buildings and their drainage. Because the Form of Bye-laws was trying to provide a comprehensive set of rules that could be applied throughout the country, they were in several respects lacking in detailed specifications and open to a variety of local interpretations. For instance, with respect to the structure of buildings the Form of Bye-laws recognised the need to regulate the thickness of walls, but left it to local authorities to determine what that thickness should be in the light of local practice.[39] Similarly, while the Form of Bye-laws reiterated the need recognised in many local Acts for external and party walls to be of brick or stone or some other strong, incombustible substance, it permitted alternatives where local authorities thought they were appropriate. It proposed the pattern adopted in the recent Metropolitan Building Act for the regulation of foundations, the controls on the use of timber in construction and the need for party walls to project above the roof line. It did not, however, adopt the form of the Metropolitan Building Act in its entirety, which is not surprising as many of the regulations drafted to suit London's needs would have been inappropriate for provincial building practices. It adopted, for example, a lower requirement for the width of streets—36 ft and 18 ft for the width of carriage-ways and non-carriage-ways respectively. It also retained features from local bye-laws which were not included in the Metropolitan Building Act, such as the control of street widths in relation to the height of the buildings adjoining them. Moreover, in certain respects the Form of Bye-laws broke new ground, notably with the extension of this relationship of building height to adjoining space to apply to the back-yards of houses.[40] The stringency of that particular regulation, like others, could however be modified if the local authority felt it was inappropriate and would lead to a 'considerable sacrifice of property'. The last statement reflected the continuing concern, particularly of provincial building regulations, with small property which produced a limited economic return. Similar caveats were allowed for in the extension of spatial regulations to the interior design of buildings, with the specification of minimum room heights and window sizes. Another new feature in the Form of Bye-laws was an acknowledgement, albeit tentatively, of the changing patterns of building and the development of new forms of construction and the use of different materials. This was particularly evident in the comparatively detailed regulations which were proposed for the control of drainage. It was quite precisely specified that drains were to be of glazed stoneware or fireclay pipes, that they were to have watertight joints set in well-puddled clay under houses and that there were to be no right-angled junctions of drain pipes either vertically or horizontally. At the same time, proper account was taken of the use of concrete in the construction of foundations and as an incombustible building material. In these ways the Form of Bye-laws embodied local experience, particularly in the Metropolis and in Liverpool under the local Act of 1846,[41] and developed and modified the regulations contained in the Towns Improvement Clauses Act.

3 Example of bye-law development in Brightside, Sheffield.
(Anthony Sutcliffe)

The Form of Bye-laws was a first attempt to provide a national structure and system for local adoption and adaptation. In many respects it was imperfect, the bye-laws proposed being in some instances too specific and in others too vague to allow for their practical application. Problems ensued when local authorities attempted to operate under these bye-laws, and it is not surprising that many authorities, particularly in larger towns and cities, continued to turn to private legislation for the means of controlling building.[42] The Form of Bye-laws was nevertheless an important development, foreshadowing the Model Bye-laws of 1877,[43] and providing a crucial link between the earlier local Acts and attempts at national

Acts and the establishment of a generally accepted system of bye-law control of building by the latter part of the nineteenth century. The earlier experience of local control, and the conflict inherent in efforts to secure some degree of uniformity and standardisation across the country in terms of national building legislation, had led to tension between the interests of local traditions and practices and the developing authority of the central controlling agency. The Local Government Act of 1858 was a significant factor in the resolution of such suspicion and apparent conflict of interests, and in the implementation of a system which balanced local concerns and national control. The Form of Bye-laws allowed for that control, along with the dissemination of national experience, within a system which left the introduction and implementation of regulations firmly in local hands. The working out of that balance between the centre and the localities, foreshadowed in 1858, was to provide over the next decades the means by which an effective and extensive pattern of bye-law control of building activity was achieved.

III The Organisation of Building Controls

The pattern of progress in urban development and housing reform during the nineteenth century was a series of well-defined spurts. The intensity of interest in the subject kept pace with the changing degree of practical activity in housing reform, which stemmed not only from legislative activity but also from both commercial and philanthropic sources. Despite the extent of the experimental work of the 1840s, it provoked little public enthusiasm, and consequently there was relatively little activity during the following decade, although urban areas continued to grow in size and overcrowding in some central districts to increase. The 1860s, however, witnessed a revival of interest in housing reform, a renewal of concern for the problems of urban life, and a steady growth of general attention to the problems relating to the laying out of estates and the planning of houses for the working class. It was during this decade that the spatial concepts were established which would produce practical changes in the future development of the Victorian town. The need to make provision for light, air and space in the layout of housing was an idea that was increasingly promoted throughout England during the 1860s and 1870s, and was to secure legislative consolidation in the Public Health Act of 1875.[44]

Ever since the 1840s there had been concern about the environmental quality of houses, in terms of their relationship to public health, and in 1857 at the first meeting of the Social Science Association the Reverend C. H. Hartshorn laid down three fundamental principles which he considered should be observed in the planning of houses for working men—aspect, light and ventilation:

> A sunny aspect gives cheerfulness to the inmates more than any artificial stimulates that can be supplied. It elevates the spirit at the commencement of the day and sends forth the workman in the pleasant courage to his labour, and besides this it imparts a genial warmth to his dwelling which no amount of heat can produce.[45]

The more spacious planning of buildings was urged, not only so as to secure the admittance of a greater degree of sunlight, but also the free circulation of fresh air. The consequences of overbuilding were clearly spelt out by George Godwin at the Social Science Congress in 1864, when he posed the question, 'What is the influence on health of the overcrowding of dwelling houses and workshops?':

> Passing the greater part of their lives deprived of that without which their is no life, pure air, a low state of health becomes chronic: they exist, do not live. Bad air takes away the appetite, depresses the spirit, lessens the vital power and predisposes to more serious diseases.[46]

The question of the circulation of fresh air was inevitably tied up with the practicalities of ventilation. Much discussion on the subject was involved with the problem of securing the most effective flow of air within a house by means of better internal layout and by the use of mechanical ventilating devices. Increasingly, however, attention was given to the circulation of air around the buildings and to the need to deal with the overall layout of an area, rather than simply improve the individual dwelling house, if the most satisfactory results were to be ensured. When H. H. Collins in 1873 asked the question, 'What provisions are required in a general Building Act so as to secure effective sanitary arrangements?', he laid down the basic requirement that all streets should be open and that alleys and cul-de-sacs should abolished:

> It should be enacted that for every house *exclusively* there should be a backyard of a minimum depth of 10 feet by the whole width of the house, and that no party fence or wall should be erected more than 7 feet high. So back-to-backs would be swept away, through ventilation provided, because passages would be constructed through houses from back to front and windows likewise. Sun, light and air, those best and prophylactic agents, which seldom penetrate the foulness and darkness of a London dwelling, would permeate throughout not only the houses but also the neighbourhood, carrying with them health to the debilitated frame, strength to the weak and doing much to solve the important problem of how best to improve the habits and homes of the poor and middle classes.[47]

Yet though reformers recognised that adequate ventilation and the abundant provision of light and air were vital prerequisites for a healthy dwelling, it was equally clear that there would have to be statutory measures to ensure the incorporation of the necessary features in the layout of housing. As the medical officer of the Mile End Old Town noted in his report of 1876:

> Water, air, light are nature's disinfectants and preventors of disease. They are abundantly provided but more meagrely and inefficiently used, and indeed are practically ignored by architects, builders, owners and occupiers . . . [48]

His complaint reflected the misgivings expressed by Dr Lethaby, the Medical Officer of Health for the City of London, as early as 1862. He reported that, though much attention had been given to the subject of sanitary improvement and the dangers inherent in the dense overcrowding of population in ill-ventilated courts and alleys, efforts at alleviation had been almost nullified by 'the passive resistance of landlords and by the sullen indifference of the poor'.[49]

Clearly there would have to be further legislative enactment to enforce the necessary sanitary and spatial reforms. In 1864, George Godwin, in his pamphlet *Another Blow For Life,* pleaded for legal interference and the application of Building Acts to ensure better standards of light, air and ventilation, and for adequate inspection in order to prevent overcrowding.[50] The implementation of satisfactory standards, it was increasingly realised, would depend on local authorities having effective and enforceable powers to guard against the overcrowding of a site and the planning of buildings so as to obscure the proper supply of light and air from others.

The realities of this situation were evident in those towns to which reference has already been made—Leeds, Manchester, Newcastle-upon-Tyne, and Sheffield. The local Acts and rudimentary building regulations introduced in these localities during the 1840s and 1850s had been very partial in their coverage and limited in their application. While important in terms of legislative development, in a practical sense they had barely touched the problems they had sought to resolve. In the early 1860s, with concern at the national level growing, there was renewed pressure at the local level for local authorities to adopt legislation and administrative procedures which reflected the standards now anticipated at the national level concerning the control and regulation of urban growth and building development. Examples of this can be found in writings of many

4 Back-to-back houses in Armley, Leeds. *(S. Martin Gaskell)*

contemporary local reformers. In Leeds, for instance, James Hole's prize essay on 'The Working Classes of Leeds', which was presented in the Town Hall in 1865, praised the bye-law system in operation in other towns and criticised the want of municipal regulations in Leeds, particularly with regard to preventing the erection of back-to-back houses with had unfortunately become almost the universal form of dwelling for the working classes in Leeds. Hole considered that the Council needed powers to regulate the type of new buildings erected:

> ... the utter powerlessness of the working man over the construction and condition of his dwelling justified municipal interference, and the municipal power had as much right to prevent these as to insist on their proper sewerage.[51]

The *Builder*, from 1860 to 1862, took up this cause with a series analysing provincial towns, in order to 'lay bare their hideousness, and suggest their improvement'. Introducing this enterprise, George Godwin commented:

> Plenty of work remains to be done—work architectural and work sanitary, work artistic and work social—notwithstanding the progress which has been made ... [52]

The surveys which followed ranged over all the factors which in any way limited the access of the urban mass to water, light and air. In doing so they highlighted the inadequacy of existing regulations and administrative control. Of Leeds, for instance, the *Builder* in its catalogue of ill-contrived streets and filthy surroundings emphasised the particular evils which had arisen through the continued absence of controls over back-to-back housing:

> The physical condition of the majority of the working classes of the town would have been good, had it been subjected to proper municipal regulations during the last 30 years. Decent houses and well drained streets are scarcely less important than good wages, or day and Sunday schools; but notwithstanding an enormous sum expended in making drains, there are many miles of houses, yards, and streets unconnected with the main drainage. In Leeds, the reprehensible mode of building cottages back-to-back, has been universally the custom, and in spite of its known evils, it is allowed to go on, no steps being even contemplated to check its growth ... Every question of convenience, or of common decency, seems sacrificed to the one consideration of getting the largest possible return for the money invested.[53]

The Leeds Local Improvement Act of 1842 had had little effect on this situation since its clauses on the layout and arrangement of buildings had been very imprecise and even though it had been much more specific in its regulation of streets and thoroughfares, the *Builder* reported that in practice, with few exceptions, the streets of the town were narrow and tortuous, badly paved and inadequately drained, filthy and poorly lighted. This was largely the consequence of inadequate enforcement of even those powers the authority possessed. A similar state of affairs, despite the emphasis of its own Improvement Act of 1837, was reported in Newcastle-upon-Tyne:

> The whole of the district [Scotswood] is laid out into long streets or terraces, about a mile long, up a steep eminence, northwards from the Tyne, and is intersected by the main arteries ... It is a most favourable site for building purposes. A good use has been made of it in the creation of neat and even handsome houses for the suburban residence of the wealthier classes. But the roads are so bad that it is impossible for carriages to approach many of them.[54]

Evasion of local controls likewise characterised the state of Manchester where the *Builder* was alarmed at the extent of the evil of cellar dwellings.[55] This was in spite of the existence of the Manchester New Streets Act of 1853 which expressly stated that no cellar made since the passing of the Act could, under any circumstances, be legally occupied as a separate dwelling, and at the same time laid down stringent conditions on the continued occupation of existing cellars. The local Act had not, however, imposed specific controls, as had been proposed in the Public Health Act of 1848; rather it had only given the Council discretionary powers to prohibit the use of any cellars as a separate dwelling. As a result, over the six years since the passage of the local Act, the number of cellars, notwithstanding their known unwholesomeness, had only declined by 176 from a total of 4,643 while the population in them had increased upwards of 1,000 persons to a total of 17,478. The *Builder* attributed this state of affairs to the fact that the Corporation was strongly influenced by ratepayers and property owners with a vested interest in this kind of housing.

Concern for individual profit and property rights accounted for the limited aspirations of most authorities in urban control and building regulation, while self-interest affected the achievement of any constructive intervention. In Sheffield, for example, the application of the Town Improvement Act was frustrated by the artisans themselves who were afraid of extra taxation on the small properties they possessed.[56] It was not just a matter for town councils, but for the inhabitants themselves to take up. Public pressure coalesced with a more general realisation of the ineffectiveness of existing national prohibitory Acts and local measures of regulation and control. In the complex process that characterised the evolution of nineteenth century social legislation, the 'pressure of intolerable facts', as revealed in this exercise of analysis and reassessment in the early 1860s, led with a certain administrative logic to the introduction of new, more effective legislation at the local level. However pragmatic the system in its derivation and development, there was within it a strong administrative momentum that ensured the enforcement of more effective and extensive regulatory controls.

Most provincial centres issued new building regulations during the course of the 1860s, and in nearly every case these were modelled, often quite closely, on the pattern established in the 1858 Form of Bye-laws. This did not necessarily mean, however,

that these were bye-laws issued under the powers of the Local
Government Act of 1858 in an administrative sense. A number of
towns continued to operate under their local Acts. It is important
therefore to distinguish between the limited impact of the Local
Government Act in terms of the number of towns adopting it, and
its far greater significance in terms of its influence on the concept and content of building legislation. Of the four case studies,
Sheffield issued new building bye-laws in 1864, Leeds and
Newcastle-upon-Tyne in 1866, and Manchester in 1867; of these
only Sheffield produced its bye-laws as a consequence of its adoption of the Local Government Act. All four examples, however, followed remarkably closely the general format of the 1858 Form of
Bye-laws, though in each case allowing for local differences and
distinctions. The Sheffield bye-laws typified this response. They
were modelled on the structure and format of the 1858 Form of Bye-
laws as regards the width and construction of streets; the structure
and stability of buildings and the prevention of fire; the sufficiency
of space about buildings and their ventilation; the drainage of buildings and the provision of conveniences; and the deposition of plans
and the powers of the Council to remove work undertaken in contravention of the bye-laws. The content of the bye-laws, however,
involved some minor modifications on points of detail: the clause
on the ventilation of house drainage was omitted; minimum room
height was set at 8 ft 6 in rather than 8 ft; the distance of timbers
from the inside face of a flue was reduced from 9 in to $4\frac{1}{2}$ in,
as was common practice in the provinces; the width of non-
carriage-ways was established at 21 ft instead of 18 ft; party walls
were not required to rise through the roof, as this was not in accord
with local building practice. Otherwise the Sheffield bye-laws took
over clauses intact from the 1858 Form of Bye-laws. This meant that
in certain significant aspects the drafting was imprecise and allowed
a variety of interpretations. For instance, as in the 1858 Form, the
bye-laws required that each dwelling house should be provided
exclusively with a minimum of 150 sq ft of open land. It did not
specify however, that such land was to be in one unit or to be open
at the rear, so there was still the danger that irregular construction
and back-to-back building was not clearly obviated. Nor was the
total space directly related to the height of the buildings, with the
result that tall buildings could still be crowded on to grossly inadequate sites.[57] Such inconsistencies were inevitable under the 1858

Form of Bye-laws; but despite these inadequacies, Sheffield's bye-laws of 1865, like comparable codes in other cities, remained virtually intact until 1889 and influenced the form of the city's major expansion.

The pattern of bye-law provision at this time was similar in most provincial towns, even those which operated under their own local Acts. The three remaining case studies displayed remarkable consistency in their approach: they accepted the general format and coverage of the Form of Bye-laws, allowing for minor deviations from the specifications laid down in that Form; especially they reflected the imprecision of the Form, not least because this enabled them to encompass local traditions and variations; occasionally they specifically legislated within the overall framework for particular local practices. The latter was most clearly demonstrated in Leeds, where the 1842 Improvement Act had given the Council power to compel a proper privy for each newly erected house, but where no summons had been issued for many years for any breach of building regulations, and where, as a result, the back-to-back system of house building had rendered this clause all but impracticable. The bye-laws of 1866 accepted this situation, and sought to control such development rather than prevent it, with the requirement that new houses of this type could not be built in blocks of more than eight (four front and four back), and yard privies had to be placed between each block. This bye-law thus established the visual and spatial standards of the normal form of development in Leeds for the later nineteenth century. On most occasions, however, sets of bye-laws merely made use of the imprecision of the 1858 Form of Bye-laws to allow for a local pattern of building which was not specifically excluded. This was the case in Newcastle-upon-Tyne where the bye-laws of 1866 included the normal clause requiring each dwelling to have a certain amount of open space around it:

> Every building hereafter erected . . . used as a dwelling-house, shall have, in the rear or at the side thereof, an open space, exclusively belonging thereto; such open space shall be equal in area to at least one-fourth of so much of the entire area of the ground occupied by, and belonging to such building and its out-offices.

This was commonly interpreted elsewhere as meaning a separate backyard in relation to the standard English self-contained terrace

5 Newcastle-upon-Tyne cottage flats built under the 1866
bye-laws. *(Martin Daunton)*

house. However, because of the lack of definition as to how that
space should be allocated, the bye-laws could encompass a different
response in the form of the Tyneside flat which was an amalgamation
of the standard English two-storey terrace and the predominant
tenement form of the North East. The bye-laws had here served to
institutionalise an earlier *ad hoc* form which had existed as a means
of dividing property.[58]

Bye-laws clearly were not the only factors influencing development, and if they were not precise then their intention could be
easily evaded or indeed contradicted. In Manchester, the newly
constituted Health Committee had seen the bye-laws of 1867 as a

means of dealing with the pressing sanitary problems of the city. But for many reasons progress was slow:

> Much ill health in the City was caused by factors outside the control of the Health Committee; the water supply was inadequate, the sewerage of the City was defective and the rivers were polluted. Many desirable reforms had therefore to wait upon the actions of other committees. . . [59]

In particular, this meant that the clauses in the bye-laws relating to the proper drainage of all new houses were largely ignored during the first ten years of their existence, as the Council failed to support the Medical Officer of Health's efforts to overcome the property owners' and ratepayers associations' continued championship of privies and ash-pits. This apparently arbitrary nature of bye-law control in Manchester occasioned the criticism of the local Society of Architects which, between 1867 and 1872, attempted to persuade the Council to codify all the sections of the various Acts of Parliament relating to building controls, and to adopt 'such building regulations as would have the effect of a building Act'.[60]

This situation was not uncommon. The building bye-laws issued by many cities during the 1860s had inherent in them the weaknesses of the 1858 Local Government Act and the Form of Bye-laws. This was the case whether the bye-laws were issued as a result of the adoption of that Act or were the consequence still of separate local legislation. The 1858 Form of Bye-laws provided the model and the standard for local action, even though many great city corporations preferred to work alone, through local Acts and with their own professional staffs. Smaller towns, without such facilities, however, benefited from the adoption of the Act in the process of creating local health government.[61] Through the means of the Act, therefore, the control of building extended to a much wider range of towns, including some small authorities which had previously possessed no powers of regulating building development.[62] The mechanism of bye-law administration became the general system of local government. Between 1858 and 1868 some 568 places adopted the Act. Adoptions averaged 30 a year during the first four years and then in 1863 and 1864 rose sharply to 90 a year. In the middle years of the decade adoptions averaged 53 a year; they fell off after 1867, as then most urban areas had local boards, with around 700 such

6 View of the backs of houses built in Ladybarn under Manchester's 1867 bye-laws. *(Manchester Public Libraries: Local History Library)*

boards active, and rural areas could now operate under the recent Sewerage Acts.

From all these authorities, between 1858 and 1871, the Local Government Act Office, which was responsible for the central administration of the Act, received for examination about 1,500 sets of bye-laws. Most of these contained provisions relating to the level, width and construction of new streets and provisions for sewerage; the structure of walls, foundations and roofs, and arrangements for securing the stability of buildings and the prevention of fire; the sufficiency of space about buildings in order to secure a free circulation of air and ventilation of buildings; the drainage of buildings and their sanitary arrangements; the closure of buildings unfit for habitation; the deposition of plans and sections by persons intending to lay out a street or construct a building. A code of bye-laws had to be approved by the Home Secretary before they could be effective, and there was consequently a persistent and growing demand from smaller local authorities, who lacked the administrative and technical resources to frame their own regulations, for guidance and even direction from the central authority in the drafting and presentation of their bye-laws. All proposals from localities were scrutinised by the staff of the Local Government Act Office prior to confirmation; they pointed out 'the variations from forms or violations of judicial decisions or statutory conditions'. As a result the Office's 'suggestions' became standards to be applied in the interests of a uniform national code and its models were usually adopted locally with 'trifling modifications'. As Royston Lambert has concluded:

> Local pressure, patent need, and individual thoroughness combined to make this apparently trivial central power a beneficial and widely-felt reality in the creation of a uniform framework for local sanitary action.[63]

That framework, however, though a considerable advance on any structure previously available, was confusing and clearly inadequate in terms of both its legal and administrative presentation. The strangely erratic scope of the 1858 Form of Bye-laws has already been noted, with some clauses being over-specific and others rather vague. An indication of this variation in approach can be seen in the respective clauses relating to room sizes, and to chimneys and fireplaces. The Form of Bye-laws was extremely precise, in the first case requiring one window in every habitable room and specifying that its openable area, clear of the frame, should be a minimum of one-tenth of the area of the room; in addition, the top of the window was to be not less than 6 ft 7 in above the floor and the upper half at least was to be openable. In contrast, while hearths and flues, chimneys and steam pipes were included, the provisions were very general, requiring only that hearths and slabs should be bedded in incombustible material and not specifying in any way the required heights for chimneys.

This ambiguity was compounded by a lack of precision in the drafting of the Form of Bye-laws. In retrospect, this can be seen as a crucial if tentative step in the centralisation and professionalisation of the mechanism for the control of buildings, but at the time, local bye-laws, which relied on it for either their legal or conceptual basis, faced problems as to interpretation and ultimately validity. The 1858 Local Government Act, the Form of Bye-laws and the work of the Local Government Act Office constituted a stage in the evolution of building control which provided not only a structure of legislation, but also the first means of enforcement through centralised supervision. The next stage was the realisation that problems could not be solved by one single piece of legislation, but required continuous clarification and re-regulation.[64] This meant in the first instance the determination, in a legal sense, of the terminology involved in building regulation. Through the 1860s and 1870s a series of court cases between individuals and local authorities established the legal definition of such issues as what was meant by a 'dwelling house', a *new* building or street, the interpretation of the building line in relation to existing buildings, the distinction between a 'street' and other passageways, the definition of the term 'party wall' and the required relationship of the back yard to a dwelling house.[65] Decisions on such matters in the courts were made effective through the directives of the Local Government Act Office and the dissemination of information in its circulars. The original lack of precision and inadequate drafting had led, however, to more serious problems with some local bye-laws making 'unreasonable' demands and invalidating themselves through their contradiction of statute law. Bye-laws, as indicated earlier, were the means of local application of a general statute; they could not enforce or direct anything contrary to that statute. A bye-law, in as much as it was additional to statute law, had to be *'certain* in its enactment, free from any ambiguity, *general* in its application, and reasonable in its requirements'.[66] The first generation of local building bye-laws often failed to meet these requirements. As the Town Clerk of Ipswich, for example, reflected on that town's bye-laws, based on the 1858 Form:

> They attempt to give Local Boards more power than they are entitled to . . . and left much to the Local Board to determine . . . This was held to be beyond the power given by the 1858 Local Government Act. An Act of Parliament could give Local Boards power to determine street widths, but a bye-law could not.[67]

By the end of the 1860s, therefore, not only were local authorities encountering serious difficulties in enforcing the bye-laws and supervising new building under construction, but there was a growing realisation that the actual bye-laws themselves were frequently legally invalid.

As a result of these problems encountered in the operation of bye-laws, not only on building but across the whole range of sanitary affairs, and because of the piecemeal and consequently conflicting way in which legislation relating to health had grown up, a Royal

Commission was established in 1869 in order to enquire into, and report on, the sanitary administration of the country. It concerned itself both with the content of legislation and the means by which that legislation was made effective. With regard to the control of buildings and streets, it was suggested that there should be an extension of the powers which urban authorities already possessed to require the deposition of plans for all new buildings, to inspect all buildings in progress, and to make bye-laws as to the line and width and sewerage of streets, and as to the thickness of the walls of buildings, the space about them and their ventilation. In the future, it was argued that they should be further empowered to enforce some of these regulations retrospectively and to license all new buildings for occupation. There should, in addition, be power of appeal to a central authority both in cases where individuals felt aggrieved by the rejection of plans and, on the other hand, where local authorities passed plans inconsistent with the bye-laws. In this area, as in sanitary matters generally, the Royal Commission considered that the various statutes needed consolidating and the means for the enforcement of the law standardising

Addressing itself particularly to the problems arising from bye-laws having been set aside as invalid by decisions of the courts,[68] the Royal Commission considered alternatives to that system of operation. There were, in effect, two main alternatives: the method of providing, by direct enactment in a statute itself, for every point on which a bye-law could be needed; or, the method of leaving the whole matter to the discretion of the local authority on each particular occasion, without attempting to lay down any general rules as to the exercise of such discretion. The problem with regard to the first method was that prohibitory clauses in a direct Act, though they had their value, could not be introduced until the problem had in fact arisen, and therefore could in no way be preventive. As to the latter method of making orders *pro re nata* on every occasion, there were advantages in freeing the local authority from supervision, but it left a somewhat arbitrary procedure. The Commission considered that on the whole bye-laws were too useful a machinery to be set aside and that no adequate substitute could be found:

> While many sanitary subjects may be specifically provided for by statute, and some may be best left to the discretion of the Local Authority, there will remain a large class to be dealt with (as now)

by means of bye-laws. We conceive the principle to be followed is this: that matters of general applicability should be included in general legislation, but that matters which require to be adapted to varying localities, or are too minute for general legislation, are the fitting subjects for bye-laws. The danger of having bye-laws set aside, upon the framing of which due care has been expended, is probably diminishing, and is likely to diminish. The experience of the last few years, and the decisions which have taken place, have thrown much light on the subject. It is everyday becoming more easy to avoid the most fatal flaws, and to accomplish with success the most necessary objects.[69]

The report of the Royal Sanitary Commission, issued in 1871, therefore confirmed the system of bye-laws with its delicate balance of local and central power characterising as the appropriate means for controlling all sanitary matters, and thereby building development. In order to make the system more effective, the Royal Commission proposed extending the practice of building bye-laws throughout the country, including rural areas; advocated the establishment of a strong and unified central body for the regulation and direction of all matters affecting local authorities; and recommended the standardisation of local authority control, with effective means of inspection and enforcement. The logical sequence to the Sanitary Commission report was achieved in the administrative and legislative developments of the subsequent five years. In 1871 the Local Government Board was established as a significant and unified department of state, supervising most of the activities of local government.[70] This rationalisation was extended to the localities in the following year when a Public Health Act established sanitary authorities which covered the whole country, and whose duties were obligatory.[71] Finally in 1875 the great Public Health Act was passed which consolidated and codified all previous sanitary legislation.

Concerned initially with administrative rationalisation, the Public Health Act of 1875 provided a logical response to the needs of sanitary reform. Its importance lay not only in its comprehensiveness, but also in its clear format and the way in which it laid down the Public Health functions and duties of local authorities. As regards the control of building development, this meant that in its essential purport it followed closely the Local Government Act of 1858, while allowing for the clarification of certain issues which the experience of the intervening period had shown to be essential. Under the terms of the Public Health Act urban authorities might make bye-laws with respect to the following matters:

(1) the level, width and construction of new streets and the provision for the sewage thereon;

(2) the structure of walls, foundations, roofs and chimneys of new buildings for securing stability and the prevention of fires and for purposes of health;

(3) the sufficiency of space about buildings to secure a free circulation of air and with respect to the ventilation of buildings;

(4) the drainage of buildings, to water closets, earth closets, privies, ash-pits and cesspools in connection with buildings, and to the closing of buildings or parts of buildings unfit for human habitation, and to prohibition of their use for such habitation.

These were the provisions of Section 34 of the Local Government Act with one significant addition; that is in Section 2, where local authorities were now able to make bye-laws not just affecting walls, but also foundations, roofs and chimneys, and to do so not just for the purpose of securing stability and the prevention of fires, but also for the purposes of health. The latter consideration involved a change in the scope of bye-laws, with greater emphasis being placed on preventive action. In the aftermath of the problems of legal definition affecting earlier bye-laws, the Public Health Act also clarified certain hitherto contentious issues: the date by which a bye-law could become effective; the period a local authority was allowed in which to approve submitted plans; the definition of categories of buildings and rebuilding, and what was meant by building lines and cellars; the clarification of offences under the bye-laws and the penalties which applied to them. With this combination of consolidation and clarification, the Public Health Act provided a comprehensive and intelligible system of controls, and formulated the framework in which subsequent building regulation was to be set.

Having extended the range of subjects for which building bye-laws could be made, the Local Government Board followed the precedent set in 1858 after the introduction of the Local Government Act, and produced a set of Model Bye-laws.[72] Like its predecessor, the Local Government Act Office, the Board was pressed by local authorities for guidance and direction on the presentation of bye-laws which were submitted for confirmation under the Act.

Conscious, however, of the limitations of the earlier model the Board took care to ensure that any new proposals would be strictly consistent with the terms of the Act and would be appropriate to the needs of all localities, which would then be able to bring their bye-laws as much as possible into uniformity under the Act. The Board therefore took the advice of the Royal Institute of British Architects and analysed current local practice.[73] Proceeding with consequent 'care and deliberation'[74] the Board delayed the publication of its Model Bye-laws until 1877. This was to ensure that, in addition to conforming to legal principles and being suitable for general operation, they should 'invite confidence' and at the same time be of a practical nature which would induce local authorities to look upon the model clauses as indicating approved methods.[75] As a result the Model Bye-laws possessed, in Harper's terms, both 'a detailed functional character' and 'a strong educative function', which made them 'nearer a technical handbook rather than mere guidelines to basic principles of performance'.[76]

The Model Bye-laws followed closely the categories provided for in the Public Health Act. First of all, in relation to new streets, it was proposed that they were to be laid out with easy gradients, and that carriage roads, which included streets exceeding 100 ft in length, were to be at least 36 ft wide. If a street was less than that length, it was to be at least 24 ft wide if it was used as an approach to buildings. For new streets the carriage-way was to be 24 ft wide at least, and the slope to be $\frac{3}{8}$ to $\frac{3}{4}$ in per foot in width; the footways were to slope $\frac{1}{2}$ in to the foot if not paved, or $\frac{1}{4}$ in if paved or asphalted. Respecting new buildings, the bye-laws provided that they should not be erected on a site filled up with faecal material, or with material impregnated with animal or vegetable refuse. Rather, the area of every house was to have a layer of asphalt or good cement concrete 6 in thick 'rammed tight'. With regard to the cementing medium, mortar of good lime and clean sharp sand was to be used or good cement. For footings, the usual regulations of the London Building Act were followed, with half of the thickness of the wall to be the measure of projection of the widest part on each side, though it was allowed that when an adjoining wall existed the projection might be omitted. Relating to external and party walls, the rules again followed those laid down by the London Building Act. Thus taking a wall 60 ft in height, with a length up to 45 ft, the thickness of the two storeys was put at 18 in and the remainder

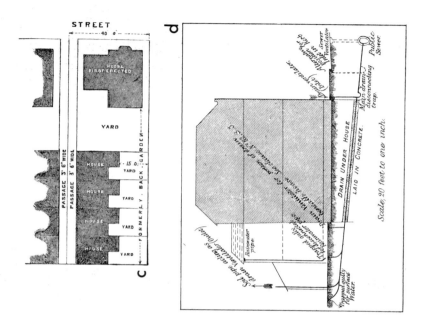

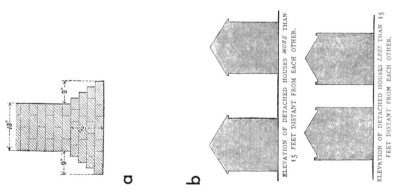

7 The implications of the model bye-laws of 1877 (illustrated in *Knight's Annotated Model Bye-laws*, 1883)
(a) Footings
(b) Requirements for parapets on certain buildings
(c) Open space in front of new buildings
(d) House drain arrangements

at $13\frac{1}{2}$ in. If the length exceeded 45 ft, one storey was to be 22 in, two storeys $18\frac{1}{2}$ in and the remainder $13\frac{1}{2}$ in. Taking an ordinary case for height up to 25 ft, with length up to 30 ft, if the building was two storeys high the thickness was to be 9 in, if more than two storeys then the requirement was $13\frac{1}{2}$ in to below the topmost storey and the remainder 9 in. The Model Bye-laws thus prescribed a complete scale of specifications. For example, if the height was in excess of sixteen times the prescribed thickness of the walls, then the thickness of each external and party wall throughout the storey was to be increased to a sixth part of the height of the storey, and the thickness of each external wall and of each party wall below that - storey was to be proportionately increased subject to the provision of piers. Every external and party wall of any storey which exceeded 10 ft in height was not to be less than $13\frac{1}{2}$ in in thickness. Where greater thickness was required in a wall which exceeded 60 ft in height and 45 ft in length, the increase might be confined to piers properly distributed, of which the collective widths amounted to a fourth part of the length of the walls. The projection of a pier was never to exceed a third of its width. For the external and party walls of buildings such as warehouses, the proposed rules followed very closely the schedule of the London Building Act; while the provisions for openings, parapets, bond-timber, chimneys and flues, holdfasts and roofs were in the main a repetition of those in that Act.

Passing on to those bye-laws relating to sanitary objects, the sufficient space around buildings and their drainage, the Model Bye-laws provided some useful specifications and clarifications. Thus, it was required that in front of every domestic building there was to be an open space of 24 ft between the frontage and the opposite lands and premises; this space was to be left quite free of obstructions, except for a portico, porch, steps, or projection not exceeding 7 ft in height. In the rear there was to be an open space of an aggregate extent of not less than 150 sq ft free from any erection, except if it was to be a water closet, privy or ash-pit. This space was to extend laterally through the entire width of the building; any opposite or adjoining premises were not to be nearer than 10 ft to any part of the building. If the building was 15 ft high, the distance was to be 15 ft; if 25 ft high the distance was to be not less than 20 ft; and if the height was 35 ft or more, the distance was to be at least 25 ft. The lowest floor of a building was to have a space of at least 3 in from the asphalt or concrete to the lowest side of the joists, and the space was to be ventilated by air bricks. Every habitable room was to have one window at least opening externally, and the total area of the window was to equal at least one-tenth of the floor area of the room; one-half of the window at least was to be constructed to open—this opening extending to the top. Every room without a fireplace was required to have efficient means of ventilation by a shaft whose sectional area should be at least 100 sq in.

Regarding drains, every damp site was to have the sub-soil drained by earthenware field pipes; suitable ventilated trapped connections were to be made; no drain was to pass under a building, except in cases where any other mode was impracticable, and when so laid it was to be in a direct line for the whole distance beneath the building, and be embedded in concrete at least 6 in thick all round, with ventilation at each end. In order to prevent the escape of foul air into any building, there had to be the possibility of disconnection by means of a shaft pipe or chamber to be provided near to a trap, with a second opening carried up by pipe as far distant from the first as possible. Closets were to be placed so that one of the sides was an external wall, with a window of not less than 2 ft by 1 ft, and one air brick was to be built in the outer wall, or there was to be a ventilating shaft to give constant ventilation. A separate cistern or flushing box was to be provided for the wc and no connection was to be allowed between any service pipes. D-traps and containers were prohibited. The variety of sanitary arrangements possible was catered for in the profusion of detailed sub-clauses in the Model Bye-laws.

This then was the first truly effective set of national building regulations produced by central government. In its composition the Local Government Board had given considerable care and attention to both sanitary requirements and the technical conditions of building. Compared with the Metropolitan Building Act as a starting point, the Model Bye-laws were more stringent in their technical requirements, though these were not as extensive in their range of controls. Following through the terms of the Public Health Act, the Model Bye-laws performed a significant feat of consolidation, and provided as such a realistic alternative to a national building Act for which there had been certain continuing professional pressure.[77] With this code, administered and controlled by the Local Government Board, the regulations relating to fire and stability, inherited from the eighteenth century, had been brought up to date and more recent regulations concerning matters of health had been incorporated. This was a substantial achievement and a constructive culmination to the pattern of previous legislation which had gradually and experimentally established increasingly sophisticated understanding and formulation of building control.

Though like most contemporary legislation the Public Health Act and the Model Bye-laws were permissive in character, they came out at a time when the importance of sanitary controls was more generally accepted than ever before. The country was ready for both the concept and the content of such procedures. In the first place, the Model Bye-laws were generally well received by the professional bodies concerned with building. There was a recognition that the complexities of building demanded specialist knowledge in the formulation and re-formulation of its regulation; this largely reconciled the architects to such an extension of interference with their aesthetic and professional freedom, though there were inevitably detailed criticisms of individual requirements. The Model Bye-laws demonstrated that it was possibe to legislate for technical issues without, in Charles Barry's words, 'vexatiously hampering the action of professional men'.[78] For architects this was a significant development of properly consolidated legislation which embraced all aspects of building control and incorporated the most practical and generally accepted standards. In the second place, the Model Bye-laws quickly established themselves as the standard of operation for local authorities in this respect. By 1882, nearly one thousand urban authorities and some 600 rural authorities had had their local building bye-laws approved.[79] The most significant developments were perhaps the extension of bye-law control to rural areas under Section 276 of the 1875 Public Health Act, and the opportunity under the terms of the consolidated legislation which the new Model Bye-laws gave towns and cities to amend and develop their regulations and bring their existing bye-laws up to the new demands of an increasingly complex building world. In some cases this meant the introduction of completely new sets of bye-laws, as in Liverpool, for example, where a new Building and Improvement Act was secured in 1882, which incorporated specifications in line with the Model Bye-laws, though suitably modified to match local practices. On the other hand, some towns and cities continued to operate under their existing legislation while introducing into this, with the agreement of the Local Government Board, certain alterations and adaptations to meet the standards set in the Model Bye-laws. For example, in 1882 Newcastle-upon-Tyne secured amendments to the existing bye-laws of 1861 with regard particularly to the line of buildings in streets. Such changes often appear to be very marginal, but they could have a significant impact on the style of building in a town by going against local custom and tightening up regulations to prevent the further construction of cul-de-sacs or back-to-backs.

In practice, this meant that, though some towns continued to operate under their own Acts or under earlier sets of bye-laws approved under the 1858 Local Government Act, most authorities by the end of the 1880s had brought their bye-laws into conformity with the national model, and thereby moved the emphasis from qualitative controls to more precisely quantitative rules. There were, of course, difficulties in implementation and inconsistencies in interpretation. Problems of supervision and inspection, the influence of vested interests and simple lack of understanding of regulations at the local level continued to frustrate the operation of building bye-laws. Furthermore, in some places, perhaps most notoriously in the West Riding with respect to back-to-back housing, local tradition ensured the continuation of undesirable modes of building permitted, or condoned, under established bye-laws.[80] In general, however, it was the great achievement of the Model Bye-laws and of the Local Government Board implementing them, that they established a level of acceptable building construction. The Board, like the Local Government Act Office before it, had an educative influence on local authorities, and this was reinforced with the regular publication by Charles Knight of updated versions of the Model Bye-laws.[81] Legal uncertainties surrounding earlier bye-law codes had been overcome and the Model Bye-laws strengthened the authority of local officials, and readily established the minimum standards for construction and layout during the remainder of the nineteenth century. As such these bye-laws have frequently been criticised as giving rise to the dreary and depressing uniformity of later Victorian urban development. The bye-laws did not, however, *require* monotonous layout and dreary design, and regulations in themselves cannot be blamed if society chooses to house its population as cheaply as possible and thereby in identical and parallel terraces of housing. What is important is that the bye-laws ensured that such houses were healthy and adequately built.

The 1875 Public Health Act and the subsequent Model Bye-laws marked a point of achievement and consolidation in the development of building controls. It was, however, the breakthrough of the 1858 Local Goverment Act that was consolidated, and the influence of that Act as subsequently operated that was built on and extended. The Public Health Act and the 1877 Model Bye-laws established as a norm what in 1858 had been made permissible. In doing this it marked the end, or at least the beginning of the end, of a notion that a uniform building Act was strictly necessary for national application; rather 'recognising correctly the need for flexibility', they retained and reinforced the bye-law form of building regulation in the future.[82] This form had arisen pragmatically and hesitantly, but through it local prejudices and politics had been effectively balanced against the advantages of nationally determined and maintained controls. As bye-laws were only permissive, final power remained with the local authority, but the Local Government Board had gained considerable power and control through its ultimate sanction of those bye-laws. It was recognised that statutory law was hardly a device best suited to handle the complex and changing world of building regulations. With power shared between central and local government, it meant that the bye-laws could at one level be standardised as though they were national regulations, and yet at the same time be flexible enough to cater for local traditions and variations. Serving in one sense to educate local opinion and elevate local standards, bye-laws were ultimately backed by the force of law in maintaining a basic level of sound building construction. If sometimes, because of the way they had developed and because of earlier legal uncertainties, bye-laws were rather too rigid and complex, they had nevertheless the great advantage that, within the parameters of the Act under which they operated, they could without undue difficulty be amended and extended in order both to clarify their intent and to cater for changing requirements in construction and design. The provisions contained in the Public Health Act were to be changed and added to by various legislative measures, but it was a reflection of the strength of the system then established that its statutory basis remained constant for fifty years and that its character and concept have continued to underpin building regulation and control. That balance has been maintained under which, as the *Builder* commented in 1877: 'Neither the Government nor the people direct public opinion or make bye-laws. It is discussion, action and reaction between the two which brings stable progress.'[83]

Source Material

Building regulations, despite their significance in the structure of local government and their fundamental impact on the environment, have been relatively neglected by historians. The most comprehensive coverage remains in an unpublished thesis: R. H. Harper, *The Evolution of the English Building Regulations, 1840–1914* (University of Sheffield PhD Thesis, 1978). This survey provides not only the most complete history of regulations during their formative years in the nineteenth and early twentieth centuries, but also analyses the factors which affected building regulations and their consequent effect on building forms in London and the provinces. This is a unique source of detailed legal and technical information as well as a clear assessment of the historical development of building regulations. Other than this, studies of the subject have been essentially catalogues of bureaucratic detail: H. C. Chanter, *London Building Law* (1946) and B. P. Davies, *Building Bye-Laws* (1935). The one attempt to bring some critical appraisal to bear is C. C. Knowles and P. H. Pitt, *The History of Building Regulation in London, 1180–1972* (1972), though even this fails to place the study of building control in a wider social and economic dimension and is concerned essentially with the history of the District Surveyors.

Students seeking practical information on the state of building law at any particular point in the nineteenth century would do best to turn to the contemporary compendiums of regulations and the glossaries on them. W. G. Lumley, *The New Sanitary Laws* (1859), and *The Public Health Act 1875* (1875); A. Ainger, *The Building Act with Notes and Cases* (1836); B. Fletcher, *Metropolitan Buildings Acts 1855–1882* (1882); C. Knight (publisher), *Annotated Model Bye-Laws* (1883), subsequent editions in 1855, 1890, 1893, 1897, 1899; W. Chance, *Building Bye-Laws in Rural Districts* (1914).

Alongside such detailed documentation students, if they are to appreciate the pressures which affected building regulations, should examine contemporary treatises and polemics on the subject. These were generally directed at the national situation, though not uncommonly investigating local information and inferences: W. Hosking,

Guide to the Proper Regulation of Buildings in Towns as a Means of Promoting and Securing the Health, Comfort and Safety of the Inhabitants (1848); G. Godwin, *Town Swamps and Social Bridges* (1859); Manchester Society of Architects, *Paper with Reference to Bye-Laws* (Manchester, 1876); W. Henman, *A Plea for the Reform of the Principles on which the Building Bye-Laws are Founded* (1904). Such monographs can be usefully supplemented by articles in periodicals, of which the *Builder* is undoubtedly the most comprehensive. Articles relating both to specific localities and particular legislation will also be found from differing viewpoints in periodicals such as: *Architectural Review; Building News; National Association for the Promotion of Social Science Transactions; Transactions of the Royal Institute of British Architects.*

The arguments with respect to the nature of building regulations and legislation are probably at their most accessible in the reports and proceedings of the official inquiries in which building control was a matter of central or indirect concern. As evidence was received from a range of authorities, such parliamentary papers frequently contain much useful information and comment on local situations. The most relevant sources for this subject include: *Report of the Select Committee on the Health of Towns* (1840); *Report of the Poor Law Commission on the Sanitary Condition of the Labouring Population of Great Britain* (1842); *Report of the Select Committee on the Regulation of Buildings and the Improvement of Boroughs* (1842); *First and Second Reports of the Royal Commission for Inquiring into the State of Large Towns and Populous Districts* (1844 and 1845); *First and Second Reports of the Royal Sanitary Commission* (1866–9 and 1871); *Report of the Royal Commission on the Housing of the Working Classes* (1884–5). Following the implementation of national legislation, such official sources are usefully supplemented by the annual reports and circulars of the government departments responsible for the relevant Acts: *The Annual Reports from the Secretary of State for the Home Department to Parliament on the execution of the Local Government Act 1858* (1859–1871); *Annual Reports of the Local Government Board* (1871 onwards).

The application of building law, at both the national and the local level, was fraught with legal complexities; these are best summarised in G. F. Chambers, *The Law Relating to Public Health and Local Government* (1883). The significance of this development was examined from one point of view in F. Clifford, *History of Private Bill Legislation* (1885). It is in respect of the legal and constitutional aspects of the subject, however, that there have been some significant recent contributions, most notably: D. N. Chester, *Central and Local Government Financial and Administrative Relations* (1951); R. J. Lambert, 'Central and Local Relations in Mid Victorian England: The Local Government Act Office 1853–71', *Victorian Studies* vi (1962), and S. Lambert, *Bills and Acts: Legislative Procedure in Eighteenth-Century England* (1971).

The study of building control in a particular locality and the implementation of building bye-laws depends essentially, however, upon access to the regulations themselves. Occasionally, these have been collected together in compendiums of local bye-laws, as for example: E. Hiley and F. C. Minshull, *Index to Local Legislation of the Corporation of Birmingham* (Birmingham, 1902); J. F. Gibson, *Newcastle-upon-Tyne Improvement Acts* (Newcastle-upon-Tyne, 1881); R. C. and W. C. Glen, *The Metropolitan Building Acts 1855–1882* (1883); W. Goldstraw, *A Manual of the Building Regulations in force in the City of Liverpool*, (Liverpool, 1902). More usually, it is necessary to have recourse to council records; a useful guide to the introduction and application of building bye-laws is to be found in P. J. Aspinall, *Building Applications and the Building Industry in Nineteenth Century Towns: The Scope for Statistical Analysis* (Birmingham, 1978). The effect of bye-law implementation is generally commented upon in the annual reports of the Medical Officers of Health or alternatively of the Highways or Improvements Committees of the various boroughs.

The implications of such control at the local level have only received limited attention from historians in such general surveys as H. Jephson, *Sanitary Evolution of London* (1901). More recently, there has been some analysis of the relationship of building control and building activity and design: C. A. Forster, *Court Housing in Kingston-upon-Hull* (Hull, 1972); R. Harper, 'The Conflict between English Building Regulations and Architectural Design 1890–1918', *Journal of Architectural Research* vi (1977).

The role of building regulations and their effect on the environment can, however, only be fully understood within the wider context of both building history and urban history. In the first instance this requires a knowledge of the now quite considerable range of secondary studies of nineteenth century housing. The most useful general survey of all types of housing throughout this period is to be found in J. Burnett, *A Social History of Housing* (1978); the housing problem and attempts at institutional reform are surveyed in a national context in E. Gauldie, *Cruel Habitations: A History of Working-Class Housing 1780–1918* (1974). An insight into local variations is provided in the two symposia: S. D. Chapman (ed), *The History of Working-Class Housing* (1971) and M. A. Simpson and T. H. Lloyd (ed), *Middle Class Housing in Britain* (1977). The problems and possibilities of different types of housing, considered as particular building phenomena, have not been widely dealt with, but two useful, if very different surveys are A. Sutcliffe (ed), *Multi-Storey Living: The British Working-Class Experience* (1974) and J. B. Lowe, *Welsh Industrial Workers Housing 1775–1875* (1977).

More recently, there has been useful examination of Victorian building from the point of view of function which has shifted the emphasis from style and design to 'the social conditions of architectural production'. The emphasis on the origin and circumstances of a building directly relates it to its social and economic context. Such an approach characterised the general survey by R. Dixon and S. Muthesius, *Victorian Architecture* (1978); this social explanation of building forms is pursued in greater detail in two studies, with sections relevant to this period: N. Pevsner, *A History of Building Types* (1976) and A. D. King (ed), *Building and Society* (1980).

Building development, however, is not only to do with individual building, or even building types, but rather with a wider spatial context. As an introduction to town planning theory and legislation in the nineteenth century, W. Ashworth's *The Genesis of Modern British Town Planning* (1954) still remains the classic study. From an architectural point of view, this has been reinforced by two books by J. N. Tarn: *Working-Class Housing in Nineteenth Century Britain* (1971), and *Five Per Cent Philanthropy: An Account of Housing in Urban Areas between 1840 and 1914* (1973). Urban development of a grander kind has been dealt with in D. J. Olsen's study of the aristocratic estates of London in *Town Planning in London; the Eighteenth and Nineteenth Centuries* (1964). This has been followed up more extensively in D. Cannadine, *Lords and Landlords: The Aristocracy and the Towns 1774–1967* (1980). Housing reforms from a planning point of view, considering development into the Garden City ideal, are dealt with in W. L. Creese's *The Search for*

Environment (1966). For consideration of the particular problems of London and the legislative response to them, there is A. S. Wohl, *The Eternal Slum. Housing and Social Policy in Victorian London* (1977). Planning, however, in the nineteenth century was the exception and it is with the control of the incoherent spread of urban building that most building regulations were concerned. The mechanics of the building industry were originally dealt with in M. Bowley, *The British Building Industry* (1966); more recent research on the subject has been incorporated in C. G. Powell, *An Economic History of the British Building Industry 1815–1979* (1981). The ramifications of the building process within the actual urban context have been analysed most clearly in J. Dyos's *Victorian Suburb* (1961). The impact of that scholarship has been seen since in numerous histories of individual towns and cities. At its best this genre is exemplified by M. J. Daunton, *Coal Metropolis: Cardiff 1870–1914* (1977), and in M. L. Thompson, *Hampstead: Building a Borough 1650–1964* (1974). Supplementing such studies are numerous theses and articles on particular aspects of local development. These are particularly helpful in describing the way in which local sources can illuminate the building process and its consequences. Such an article is J. Smith, 'Ten Acres of Deansgate in 1851', in *The Transactions of the Antiquarian Society of Lancashire and Cheshire* (1980). It could be replicated for many other towns; clearly it is not possible to itemise all such studies. For those interested, probably the most comprehensive and accessible bibliographies of recent research and publications in this field are to be found in the *Urban History Yearbooks* (1974 onwards).

However, the historian concerned with the impact of bye-laws at the local level must in the end undertake detective work himself. The study of the advancing progress of a town, both economically and physically, depends on the dating of buildings; ordnance surveys and town maps provide a basic framework within which census returns and directories, as well as rate-books, provide an increasingly precise picture of development. The use of buildings and their social status is again indicated in the census returns, in the case of housing, and more generally and regularly in the directories, as well as in the local press. The pattern of building and the influence of individuals can be pieced together through the relationship and interaction of financiers, builders and the ultimate owners of property. In this the bye-laws themselves provide an important source of information since they required the deposition of plans with local councils for their approval. Most municipal building departments will have kept plans and specifications, and these give a picture not just of the original image of buildings, but indicate also the impact of the bye-laws on the design and layout of them. The unravelling of all this information is a complex process, not least because much of the material is fragmentary and many things remain unrecorded.[84] In the end, however, the urban historian concerned to understand the impact of bye-law control on building and its implications for the appearance of towns, has no alternative but to walk the streets in order both to observe and record the reality in bricks and mortar of otherwise distant bureaucratic devices.

Notes

(Place of publication given when other than London.)

1. The towns selected for examination and illustration in this study
   are Leeds, Manchester, Newcastle-upon-Tyne and Sheffield.
   These have been chosen not only because they were all, in their
   different ways, to the fore in the urban expansion of Victorian
   England, but also because they reflect a range of local problems and traditions, as well as a variety of legislative and administrative responses. They exemplify the way provincial towns
   developed their bye-laws to control buildings, compared with
   the continuing dependence of the capital on its own Building
   Acts.
2. W. G. Lumley, *The New Sanitary Laws* (1859), p. vii.
3. G. F. Chambers, *A Digest of the Law Relating to Public Health
   and Local Government* (1881), pp. 22–3.
4. 5 & 6 W.4 c.76 and 1 & 2 V. cap. 24.
5. The scope of this activity is clearly and thoroughly identified
   in: F. Clifford, *A History of Private Bill Legislation* (1877).
6. 14 Chas. II cap. 2.
7. 14 Geo. III cap. 78.
8. F. Clifford, *op. cit.*, i, p. 291.
9. J. L. & B. Hammond, *The Age of the Chartists* (1930), p. 309.
10. *Second Report of the Royal Commission on the State of Large
    Towns and Populous Districts*, P. P. 1844, xviii, p. 75.
11. An indication of the most useful of these reports and the ways
    in which they can be of value in the study of the history of
    nineteenth century building and building control at the local
    level is given in the guide to source material (see p. 53).
12. Lords Sessional Papers (1842), xxvii, p. 240.
13. These conditions are dealt with, along with examples from other
    towns, in J. Burnett, *A Social History of Housing 1815–1970*
    (1978), pp. 54–76.
14. Useful evidence from this source can be found both in the
    writings of medical men, such as J. P. Kay, *The Moral and
    Physical Condition of the Working Classes* (1832), and in the
    official reports of medical officers at both the local and national

level, such as the annual reports on Liverpool of W. H. Duncan, the first medical officer of health to be appointed in 1846, and the detailed studies of Southwood Smith, Physician to the London Fever Hospital, contained in the Reports of the Poor Law Commission in 1838 and 1839.

15. *Fifth Annual Report of the Poor Law Commission 1839, Appendix C*, No. 2: 'Report on the prevalance of fever in twenty Metropolitan Unions or Parishes during the year ended 20 March 1838' by T. Southwood Smith M.D., Physician to the London Fever Hospital.

16. *Royal Commission on the State of Large Towns*, etc., evid. para. 988.

17. *Select Committee Report on the Health of Towns, 1840*, P. P. 1840, xi, p. xv.

18. This recommendation should be compared with the specifications included in later legislation and particularly the Form of Bye-laws of 1858 (see p. 24) and the Model Bye-laws of 1877 (see p. 44).

19. *Hansard*, lvi, 29 Jan. 1841, p. 138.

20. 5 and 6 Will. IV, cap. 76.

21. *Hansard*, lvii, April 1841, p. 806 and 23 April 1841, p. 1018.

22. *Select Committee Report on the Regulation of Buildings and the Improvement of Boroughs, 1842*. P.P. 1842, x.

23. *Ibid.*, pp. 136–39.

24. 7 and 8 Vic. cap. 84.

25. W. Hosking, *A Guide to the Proper Regulation of Buildings in Towns* (1848).

26. E. P. Hennock, *Fit and Proper Persons* (1973), p. 5.

27. 7 Will. IV & 1 Vic. cap. 172.

28. 5 and 6 Vic. cap 104.

29. 8 and 9 Vic. cap. 141.

30. In Leeds these were laid down as 30 ft for carriageways and 20 ft for foot passage; in Manchester only a minimum width of 24 ft was specified. For comparison with the Metropolitan Building Act, see p. 15, and with Lord Normanby's Bill, see p. 13.

31. W. G. Lumley, *op cit.*, p. x.

32. 10 and 11 Vic. cap. 34.

33. 11 and 12 Vic. cap. 63.

34. 5 Vic. cap. 44. The context of this Act is usefully dealt with in J. H. Treble, 'Liverpool Working-Class Housing, 1801–1851'

in S. D. Chapman (ed), *The History of Working-Class Housing* (1971), pp. 165–220. Treble summarises the powers which the Improvement Act gave the Health Committee over the development of the local environment:

> In future no courts were to be built unless they were at least 15 ft wide and open at one end, while new streets had to conform to a minimum width of 24 ft. Each new house was required by law to have at least one room that was 100 sq ft in area. In addition, every room with the exception of the garret was to be not less than 8 ft high and to possess windows of uniform size. Equally important, all court houses, including those already in existence, were to be paved and drained at their owners' expense.

35. 21 and 22 Vic. cap. 98.
36. 21 and 22 Vic. cap. 97.
37. R. Lambert, 'Central and Local Relations in Mid-Victorian England: The Local Government Act Office 1858–71', *Victorian Studies*, vi. (1962), p. 125.
38. 'Forms of Bye-laws prepared in the Local Government Act Office and issued to Local Boards of Health under the Public Health Act 1848 and Local Boards established under the Local Government Act 1858', in *First Annual Report by the Secretary of State for the Home Department to Parliament on the Execution of the Local Government Act 1858*, P.P. 1859 xi, second series, pp. 30 *et seq.*
39. What this meant in practice can be seen, for example, in the Bye-laws introduced in Newcastle-upon-Tyne in 1866: The external walls of every building hereafter to be erected, other than out-offices attached to any building, shall, if of brick, be of the following minimum thicknesses, namely:
Of every such building of one storey in height, fourteen inches.
Of every such building of two storeys in height, fourteen inches.
Of every such building of three storeys in height—for the first storey, eighteen inches; above, fourteen inches.
Of every such building of more than three storeys in height—for the three top storeys, fourteen inches; for all other storeys, eighteen inches.

Of every basement of every building, two inches greater thickness than the wall immediately above such basement.

If of stone, the walls shall, in each case above mentioned, be three inches thicker.

All external walls of out-offices and yard boundary walls, hereafter erected, shall, whether of brick or stone, be at least nine inches thick.

All party walls of buildings, hereafter erected, and all division or internal walls of such buildings, to support joisting or other timbers, shall be at least nine inches thick.

40. Compare this with the clause relating to space about buildings in the Metropolitan Building Act of 1844 which specified only that all houses were to have backyards of 100 sq ft minimum, which were to be enclosed with no buildings thereon. This formulation, which did not relate the amount of open space at the rear of a building to its height, was commonly used in the first bye-laws of many provincial towns.

41. 9 and 10 Vict., cap. 127.

42. Examples of the response of different towns is given in the next chapter, but it is important to note the implications of this for the study of building regulations at the local level. While those towns adopting the Local Government Act will be listed in the reports of the Local Government Act Office and their resulting bye-laws will be generally in conformity with the Form of Bye-laws, those towns and cities bringing in private legislation can only be followed up through the relevant local Acts. The latter have been usefully catalogued in: HMSO, *Index to Local and Personal Acts (1801–1947)* (1949).

43. See Chapter III, p. 44.

44. 38 and 39 Vic. cap. 98.

45. *Transactions of the National Association for the Promotion of Social Science* (1857), p. 440.

46. *Ibid.* (1864), p. 514.

47. *Ibid.* (1973), p. 455.

48. Mile End Old Town Officer of Health, Annual Report, 1876, quoted in H. Jephson, *The Sanitary Evolution of London* (1907), p. 227.

49. *The Times*, 29 April 1862.

50. G. Godwin, *Another Blow for Life* (1864), p. 94.

51. J. Hole, 'The Working Classes of Leeds', essay of 1865

reprinted as appendix in his *Homes of the Working Classes* (1866), p. 125.

52. The *Builder*, xviii (1860), p. 729.
53. *Ibid.*, xviii (1860), p. 809.
54. *Ibid.*, xix (1861), p. 243.
55. *Ibid.*, xx (1862), pp. 813–14. 833–34.
56. *Ibid.*, xix (1862), pp. 641–42, 675–77.
57. This is a good indication of how significant is the actual drafting of bye-laws. In any study of the effect of bye-laws on the nature of building and layout it is essential to give very close attention to the precise wording used. It is perhaps therefore worth quoting in full the actual clause in the Sheffield Bye-laws which had the consequences indicated:

> Every building to be erected and used as dwelling house shall have in the rear, or at the side thereof, an open space exclusively belonging thereto, to the extent at least of 150 square feet, free from any erection thereon above the level of the ground. And the distance across such open space between every such building and the opposite property at the rear or side shall be ten feet at least; if such building be two stories in height above the level of such open space, the distance across shall be 15 feet; if such building be three stories, it shall be 20 feet; if more than three stories, 25 feet. When, however, through ventilation of such open space is secured, or when on the rebuilding of houses within the town these dimensions cannot be adhered to without considerable sacrifice of property, they may be modified in special cases at the discretion of the Council.

58. M. J. Daunton, *Housing Peculiarities: The North East of England, 1850–1914*, Unpublished paper given to the Planning History Group, March 1979.
59. A. Redford, *The History of Local Government in Manchester* (1939), pp. 411–12.
60. The *Builder*, xxx (1872), p. 953; xxxi (1873), p. 506.
61. For instance, the list of towns adopting bye-laws under the Local Government Act in its first year of operation includes: Skipton, Bath, Nuneaton, Dartford, Salisbury, Nantwich, Eastbourne, Altrincham and Boston.
62. An indication of those towns which brought forward bye-laws under the Act can be obtained from the annual reports pre-

sented by the Secretary of State for the Home Department to Parliament on the execution of the Local Government Act. These run from 1859 to 1871 when they were superseded by the Annual Reports of the Local Government Board. They included lists of towns which during the preceding year adopted the Act, or part of the Act, or introduced bye-laws under the Act. Not only are these reports a very useful guide as to which individual towns were acting under this legislation, but also a valuable overall picture of the kind of towns involved.

63. R. Lambert, *op. cit.*, p. 131.
64. Such a sequence of events has been identified in several models of the growth of government control and state intervention in the nineteenth century. See for example: W. C. Lubenow, *The Politics of Government Growth* (1971); O.O.G.M. MacDonagh, *The Passenger Acts: A Pattern of Government Growth* (1961); H. Parris, *Constitutional Bureaucracy* (1969).
65. G. F. Chambers, *op. cit.*, pp. 447–461, 497–99.
66. R. H. Harper, *The Evolution of the English Building Regulations 1840–1914*, (Unpublished PhD Thesis, University of Sheffield, 1978), p. 132. See also, W. G. Lumley, *An Essay on Bye-Laws* (1877), *passim*.
67. Royal Sanitary Commission, *First Report* (1869), A. A. 1413–15.
68. The most comprehensive summary of relevant problems and legal cases is to be found in G. F. Chambers, *A Digest of the Law relating to Public Health and Local Government* (1881). From the many cases where individuals contested the powers of local authorities, it becomes clear that the questions which arose most frequently concerning the validity of bye-laws were not to do with whether they were properly formulated, but rather whether they were *ultra vires* and overstepped their limits altogether. The problems encountered therefore were very much to do with enforcement and often arose from poor drafting. In many cases the bye-laws were challenged owing to a lack of clarity about their date of imposition and the nature of the penalties that could be enforced under them. Court decisions had a significant effect on the actual operation of the bye-laws in a particular locality, and in order to check on these there is really no alternative to following through references to that locality in the *Law Journal* or the *Law Times*.
69. Royal Sanitary Commission, *Second Report* (1871), p. 53.

70. 34 and 35 Vic. cap. 70.
71. 35 and 36 Vic. cap. 79.
72. Local Government Board, *Seventh Annual Report 1877–8* (1878), Appendix A, 'Model Bye-Laws as to New Streets and Buildings 1877'.
73. The *Builder*, xxxiv (1876), pp. 607–8. *RIBA Transactions,* xxvii (1877–78), p. 294.
74. Local Government Board, *Sixth Annual Report 1876–7* (1877), p. lx.
75. Local Government Board, *Seventh Annual Report 1877–8,* (1878), p. xcviii.
76. R. H. Harper, *op. cit.,* p. 276.
77. This theme was developed in two papers entitled 'General Building Regulations for the United Kingdom' given at the RIBA General Conference in 1876. See, the *Builder,* xxxiv (1876), p. 594.
78. The *Builder*, xxxv (1877), p. 1124.
79. An indication of those towns and cities and rural areas adopting the Public Health Act and securing sets of bye-laws or amendments to existing bye-laws can be found in the Annual Reports of the Local Government Board. Though the Board was responsible for a whole range of local matters, its reports do indicate the nature of the bye-laws approved for different places. In order to study the precise nature of the regulations introduced, however, it is necessary to follow these agreements through in either the Papers of the Local Government Board at the Public Record Office or in the minutes and papers of the relevant committees of the local authority concerned.
80. F. W. Barry, and P. G. Smith, *Joint Report on Back-to-back Houses to the Local Government Board* (1888), *passim. Building News,* lv (1888), p. 256.
81. C. Knight (publisher), *Annotated Model Bye-Laws,* 1st edn 1883; 2nd edn 1885; 3rd edn 1890; 4th edn 1893; 5th edn 1897; 6th edn 1899.
82. R. H. Harper, *op. cit.,* p. 254.
83. The *Builder*, xxxv (1877), p. 970.
84. A more detailed account of the problems involved in the study of nineteenth century urban housing, and of the range and character of the sources available is to be found in the author's chapter on 'Urban Housing in the Nineteenth Century' in A. Rogers, *Group Projects in Local History* (1977).